REAL PUB FOOD

Absolute Press

First published in Great Britain in 2001 by
Absolute Press
Scarborough House
29 James Street West
Bath BA1 2BT
England
Phone 44 (0) 1225 316013
Fax 44 (0) 1225 445836
E-mail info@absolutepress.demon.co.uk
Website www.absolutepress.demon.co.uk

Project Editor Meg Avent

Food Editor Hilaire Walden
Copy Editor Deborah Flower

Book Design Matt Inwood
Photography Carlo Chinca

Publisher Jon Croft

The editor and publisher would especially like to thank Sally and Kirk Ritchie of
The Fox Inn in Lower Oddington, and Tom Norrington Davies and Mike Belben of
The Eagle in London, for their kind and generous help towards the production of this book.

All the photographs that feature in *Real Pub Food* were taken on the premises
of The Fox Inn and The Eagle.

A catalogue record of this book is available from the British Library

ISBN 1 899791 19 1

Printed and bound in Italy by Lego Print

CONTENTS

INTRODUCTION

Even ten years ago a book such as *Real Pub Food* would have been unthinkable. It was 'Pub Grub' way back then. Deep fried scampi, caught straight from the freezer that very second and then on to your table in the tinkling of a microwave's 'ping'. And to follow? Perhaps Duck à l'Orange, in a free-range vacuum-packed plastic bag, snipped open, heated through and plated in an instant. Maybe some Oven Chips as a side dish. Then the pièce de resistance: a heart-stopping wedge of Black Forest Gateau, smothered in piped synthetic cream. Gassy beer and dubious brand name wines to accompany. A very British horror story.

But now the world is changing fast in the kitchens of so many of the pubs and inns across Britain. Some of the most talented restaurant chefs working today have decided that the perfect place for them to really show off their skills is in the more relaxed, less pretentious environment of a traditional British pub. Some call these places 'gastropubs', though most of the chefs working in them hate the name, others just think of them as really great places to enjoy wonderful food and drink without all the stuffiness and formality of restaurant eating.

It was The Eagle in Farringdon Road in London that paved the way for a unique style of London real pub food: mismatched furniture, no booking policy, democratic eating, dishes with gutsy Mediterranean flavours. A place where you grabbed a table when you could. The more traditional country inns looked to the likes of The Angel in Hetton in North Yorkshire that had been serving amazing food for so many years to so many. In 2001 the unthinkable happened: an English pub received a Michelin Star for its cooking – The Stagg Inn in Titley in Herefordshire. The world was being turned upside down and anything seemed possible....

These are exciting times for British food and it seems that in the pubs and inns across the land a kind of English version of the French bistro is beginning to emerge. Perhaps the time will come when just to stop off at random at an inn serving real pub food, weary after a long day's travelling, will be enough to virtually guarantee you a meal of quality – that would be a great day indeed. Perhaps the publication of this book suggests that that great day may not be so very far away.

Of course, this book would not be possible without all the enthusiastic help and encouragement of the chefs and licensees of the pubs and inns featured here, who have given so many of their best and most popular recipes for publication. For all this, the editor and publisher of Real Pub Food give their sincere thanks.

SALOON

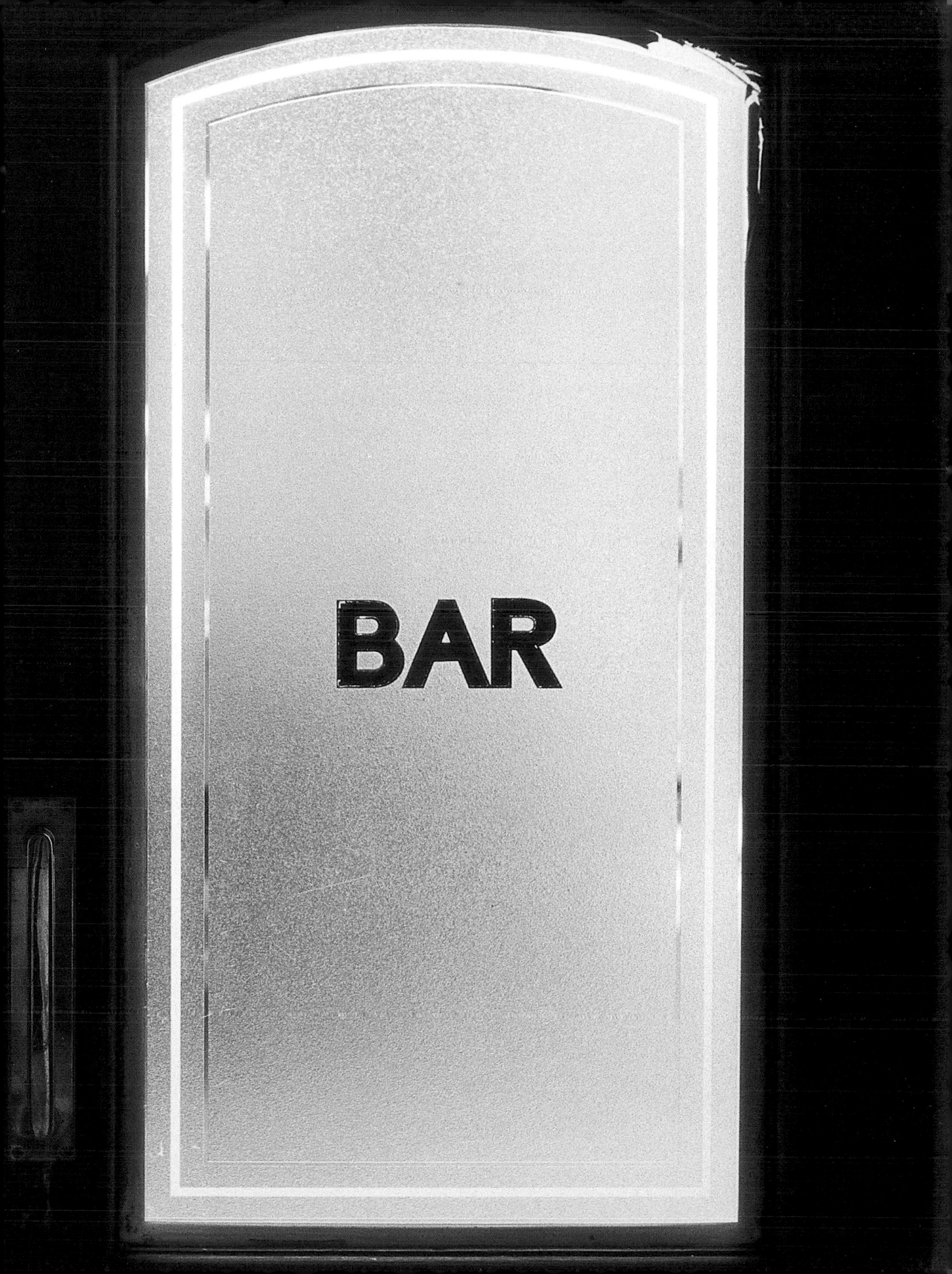
BAR

THE ANGEL
Hetton, North Yorkshire

Denis Watkins' and John Topham's legendary Yorkshire pub has been serving wonderful food for many years to discerning food lovers. Over 400 years old, The Angel was one of the first pubs to push the boundaries of expectation of pub food with its mixture of modern European and more traditional English dishes, perfectly executed and served in lovely surroundings with gorgeous views of Rylestone Fell.

Starter	Little Moneybags

A treasure of seafood with a rich shellfish sauce.

50g/2oz clarified butter, melted
50g/2oz mixed leek, yellow and red pepper and courgette, cut into fine julienne
4 chives
50g/2oz salmon fillet, skinned and cut into 5mm/^{1}/$_4$" cubes
50g/2oz cod fillet, skinned and cut into 5mm/^{1}/$_4$" cubes
50g/2oz halibut fillet, skinned and cut into 5mm/^{1}/$_4$" cubes
8 queen scallops
500g/1lb 2oz fresh prawns

4 sheets of Fleur de Bric pastry, or filo
12 tarragon leaves
salt and pepper

For the Shellfish Sauce
1^1/$_2$ tbsp vegetable oil
shells from the prawns
^{1}/$_2$ fennel bulb, chopped
1 carrot, chopped
50g/2oz leeks, chopped
4 shallots, chopped
1 garlic clove

1 sprig of tarragon
1 sprig of thyme
1 bay leaf
50ml/2fl oz brandy
115ml/4fl oz dry white wine
50g/2oz tomato flesh
1^1/$_2$ tbsp tomato purée
600ml/1pt 2fl oz fish stock
225g/8oz chilled unsalted butter, diced
pinch of cayenne pepper
salt and pepper

Start the moneybags: heat a little butter in a frying pan or wok and stir-fry the vegetables until they just start to soften. Remove from the pan and allow to cool completely. Blanch the chives in boiling water for 10 seconds. Refresh in chilled water, drain and set aside.

To make the sauce, heat a pan until smoking. Add the oil and prawn shells and cook for 5 minutes. Stir in the vegetables, garlic and herbs and cook for another 5 minutes. Pour in the brandy and, using a long, lighted taper, set it alight. Add the white wine, tomato flesh, tomato purée and fish stock. Bring to the boil and simmer for 30 minutes. Pass through a fine sieve into a clean pan and boil until reduced by two thirds. Whisk in the butter, a few pieces at a time. Add cayenne and seasoning to taste.

While the sauce is cooking, finish the moneybags: divide the vegetables and seafood into four equal portions. Working with one sheet of pastry, put a portion of seafood in the centre, then a mound of vegetables and finally 3 tarragon leaves and seasoning. Bring up the outsides of the pastry, crimp the edges together above the fish mixture and secure with a chive strip. Bake in a preheated oven 200°C/400°F/gas 6 for 10 minutes until the pastry is golden brown.

To serve, place a moneybag in the centre of each plate and spoon the shellfish sauce around.

Serves 4

Main	Confit of Lamb and Vegetables

1 shoulder of lamb (about 2kg/4lb), deboned
2.5kg/5 1/2lb duck fat or enough when melted to completely cover the lamb when cooking
50g/2oz pig's caul
mashed potatoes, to serve

For the Dry Marinade
50g/2oz sea salt
3 garlic cloves, chopped
4 shallots, chopped
leaves from 6 sprigs of thyme
leaves from 6 sprigs of rosemary
1 tsp crushed juniper berries
1 tsp crushed allspice berries

1 tsp black peppercorns

For the Confit of Vegetables
You will need 6 small Chinese take-away, or similar, foil dishes and lids
6 button onions
6 shallots
12 turned carrots
6 turned courgettes
6 button mushrooms
6 strips of celery, cut diagonally into 2cm/3/4" lengths
6 garlic cloves
6 asparagus spears
6 shiitake mushrooms

6 tbsp clarified butter
6 1/2 tsp caster sugar
12 black peppercorns
6 bay leaves
6 sprigs of thyme
6 pinches of salt

For the Lamb Jus
1 garlic clove
1 shallot, chopped
4 sprigs of thyme
4 sprigs of rosemary
2 tbsp olive oil
150ml/5fl oz red wine
1l/1 3/4pt lamb stock
1 tbsp redcurrant jelly

Mix all the marinade ingredients together.

Lay the shoulder open, skin side down, on a chopping board. Rub with the marinade and leave in a fridge for 12-24 hours. The meat starts to be slightly cured and takes on the flavours.

Wash off the marinade and pat the lamb dry with paper towels. Roll up the shoulder tightly and wrap with the caul fat and string. Place in a deep dish and cover with melted duck fat. Bake in a preheated oven at 150°C/300°F/gas 2 for 3-4 hours until the meat is very soft (the fat should hardly bubble at all throughout the cooking). Carefully remove the lamb from the fat. Drain on a wire rack and allow to cool completely. Place in the fridge for 12 hours to set the meat. Then cut the shoulder into 2-3cm/3/4-1 1/4" roundels.

To make the confit of vegetables, divide all the ingredients equally among the foil dishes. Cover with the lids, foil side up to slow down cooking. Cook the lamb and vegetables in a preheated oven at 190°C/375°F/gas 5 for 16-20 minutes. The lamb should be crisp and the vegetables just tender.

Meanwhile, make the lamb jus: cook the garlic, shallot, thyme and rosemary in the olive oil for 5 minutes. Add the wine, boil until reduced by half then add the lamb stock and reduce to a sauce consistency. Strain then return to the pan and whisk in the redcurrant jelly and check the seasoning.

To serve, put a quenelle of mashed potatoes in the centre of each plate. Pour the vegetables and juices from the foil dishes over the potato. Place the lamb on top and add the lamb jus.

Serves 6

Dessert | Sticky Toffee Pudding

50g/2oz unsalted butter,
  softened
150g/5oz caster sugar,
  plus extra for sprinkling
1 egg, beaten
200g/7oz self-raising flour

1 tsp baking powder
150g/5oz chopped dates
1 tsp bicarbonate of soda
300ml/1/2pt boiling water

For the Caramel Sauce
(If you like lots of sauce just
  increase the amounts)
250g/9oz brown sugar
250ml/9fl oz double cream
250g/9oz unsalted butter

Cream the butter and sugar until pale. Add the egg and beat well. Stir in flour and baking powder.

Put the dates and bicarbonate of soda in a bowl and pour over the boiling water. Mix thoroughly into the creamed mixture. Thoroughly butter a deep baking tray 30x20x12cm/12x8x5" and sprinkle with sugar. Pour in the pudding mixture and bake in a preheated oven at 180°C/350°F/gas 4 for 35-40 minutes.

To make the sauce, simmer the brown sugar, cream and butter in a pan until caramel coloured. Fork the top of the sticky toffee pudding and pour over the caramel sauce.

Serves 4-6

And... | Pacific Style Squid Salad

For the Dressing
2 red chillies, preferably bird's
  eye, halved
750ml/1$\frac{3}{4}$pt rice vinegar
250g/9oz sugar
juice of 2 limes

For the Squid
500g/1lb 2oz cleaned squid
  tubes, cut into 7cm/2$\frac{3}{4}$"
  squares

4 tbsp plain flour
1 tbsp chilli powder
1 tbsp onion powder
1 tbsp garlic salt
1$\frac{1}{2}$ tsp salt
1$\frac{1}{2}$ tsp ground black pepper

1 green pepper, cut into julienne
  strips
1 yellow pepper, cut into julienne
  strips

1 red pepper, cut into julienne
  strips
1 carrot, cut into julienne strips
4 spring onions, cut into julienne
  strips
1 small red onion, thinly sliced
1 red chilli, thinly sliced
leaves from 1 bunch of
  coriander
vegetable oil, for deep frying

To make the dressing, put the chillies into a saucepan with the vinegar and sugar. Simmer for 20 minutes until the mixture has reduced to a syrup. Add the lime juice, strain and leave to cool.

Score the squid with a sharp knife to make a criss-cross pattern but do not cut too deeply. Mix the flour, chilli powder, onion powder, garlic salt, salt and black pepper. Heat the vegetable oil to 180°C/350°F. Dip the squid into the seasoned flour until each piece is well coated. Add to the oil in batches and fry for about 1 minute until the flour crust is crisp. Drain on paper towels and cut into slices. Mix the vegetables, chilli and coriander leaves together and add the squid. Pour over dressing, toss and serve.

Serves 4

And...   Provençal Fish Soup

2 tbsp olive oil
zest of $^1/_2$ orange
2 tsp saffron filaments
1 red chilli
1 tbsp garlic, chopped
2 tsp ginger, chopped
1 bay leaf
2 large onions, diced
1 large courgette, diced
2 large carrots, diced
2 large leeks, diced

$^1/_3$ head of celery, diced
1 fennel bulb, diced
several parsley stalks
300ml/$^1/_2$pt white wine
1.75l/3pt fish stock
3 red peppers, roasted, peeled
   and chopped
1 x 400g/14oz can plum
   tomatoes
salt and pepper
500g/1lb 2oz sea bream fillets,

   chopped
500g/1lb 2oz grey mullet fillets,
   chopped
500g/1lb 2oz cod fillets,
   chopped
300g/10oz fresh mussels
1 x 200g/7oz squid, cleaned
   and sliced
coriander and toasted croutons,
   to serve

In a hot, large, heavy pan infuse the olive oil with the orange zest, saffron, chilli, ginger and bay leaf for 2 minutes. Add the onion, courgette, carrots, leeks, celery, fennel and parsley stalks and cook over a medium heat for 10 minutes. Add the white wine and bring to the boil. Boil for 2 minutes and add the fish stock, red peppers and tomatoes. Return to the boil then reduce the heat and simmer for 45-60 minutes. Cool slightly then blend the soup in a food processor and pass through a fine sieve.

Pour back into the pan and bring to the boil. Check the seasoning. Add the diced fish, mussels and squid and simmer for 3-4 minutes until the mussels open. Discard any mussels that do not open. Add plenty of coriander and serve with toasted croutons.

Serves 6

THE ATLAS
Seagrave Road, London SW6

The Atlas in Earls Court, brothers Richard and George Manners' first pub venture, proved an instant success: they have now opened another pub in Battersea, The Fox and Hounds (see page 56). Richard handles the front of house and the business side of things while George, who used to cook at the Eagle in Farringdon Road (see page 42), moves between the two pubs overseeing the kitchens and cooking as much as he can. Theirs is Mediterranean influenced food of the highest order, served in relaxed surroundings by people with a passion for what they are doing.

Starter	Smoked Haddock Aïoli on Toast

An alternative brunch-style dish that's easy to make yet packed with savoury flavour, and it will keep for a couple of days in the fridge. While its origins lie in the south of France, a peppery Tuscan olive oil seems to yield a richer, spicier taste.

1 glass of white wine	juice of $1/2$ lemon	2 sprigs of flat leaf parsley
5 cloves	1 whole egg	1 sprig each of chives and dill
4 bay leaves	1 egg yolk	salt and pepper
1 sprig of rosemary	about 150ml/5fl oz extra virgin	toasted rustic bread and a lightly
450g/1lb smoked haddock	olive oil	dressed rocket salad, to serve
2 garlic cloves	1 tbsp capers	

Pour the wine into the saucepan and add the cloves, bay and rosemary. Bring to simmering point and add the haddock. Poach for 5 minutes then strain and leave to cool. Using your fingers, break the haddock into chunky flakes being sure to remove any bones and pieces of skin.

Meanwhile, mix the garlic, lemon juice, whole egg and egg yolk in a food processor. With the motor running, very slowly trickle in the olive oil until the mixture takes on a thickish consistency that won't fall off the back of a spoon. If it gets too thick, loosen with a couple of tablespoons of boiling water. Transfer to a mixing bowl. Stir in the capers, parsley, chives and dill. Finally, gently stir in the smoked haddock flakes so the fish doesn't fall completely to pieces.

Serve on the toasted rustic bread with the rocket salad on the side.

Serves 6

Main	**Sicilian Beef Casserole**

In my opinion, this is the best of the wintry beef casseroles, combining the gamey wild flavours of porcini with the sweetness of shallots and Marsala. You will need the widest casserole you can get your hands on to allow uniform cooking. My mother made better roast potatoes than I have ever eaten in any restaurant in my life, and below is her recipe.

75ml/3fl oz olive oil
1kg/2lb stewing beef, cut into
    5cm/2" pieces
salt and pepper
100g/3$^1/_2$oz butter
450g/1lb small shallots

1 large white onion, finely diced
2 carrots, finely diced
2 celery sticks, finely diced
1 leek, finely diced
handful of dried porcini
leaves from 4 sprigs of rosemary

$^1/_2$ bottle Marsala
1kg/2lb waxy potatoes,
    quartered
bunch of rocket, to garnish
rock salt, to serve

Pour 50ml/2fl oz of olive oil into a large casserole and heat it until it starts to smoke. Season the beef, add to the casserole and brown on all sides, making sure there is no burning on the bottom of the pan. Remove the beef and keep warm.

Add half the butter to the casserole, followed by the shallots. When browned, add the diced vegetables and fry until they are soft and have released their sweetness. Now add the porcini and rosemary, gently stirring so as not to break the shallots.

Finally, return the beef to the pot, making sure all the ingredients are evenly distributed across the base. Pour in the Marsala, cover with a lid and put in a preheated oven at 190°C/375°F/gas 5 for 1$^1/_2$ hours. When removed from the oven, put on the lowest heat on the hob with the lid off to slightly reduce the dark, juicy liquid. The smell as you lift the lid will fill your house and might well rescue any lunch guest who might be thinking of turning vegetarian – or, alternatively, push them over the edge completely.

While the pot is still in the oven, put the remaining butter into a roasting tin and put in the oven to heat. Bring the potatoes to the boil. Drain them immediately and return to the pan. Shake them about to roughen the edges. Tip the semi-fluffy potatoes into the roasting tin. The butter must be hot when you add the potatoes, or else it's big trouble: the potatoes will weld themselves to the tin and will not only disappoint your guests but they will cast a veil of chagrin over the most zealous of washer-uppers. Roast for about 40 minutes, agitating the tin every 10 minutes.

To serve, put 4 pieces of meat evenly spaced on each large plate. Spoon the vegetables and sauce from the pan over the meat and put 4 potatoes in the gaps. Garnish with a few sprigs of rocket. Sprinkle with rock salt.

Serves 4

Dessert | Coco's White Chocolate and Almond Cake

This pudding is seriously naughty. Seriously. The recipe is a bastardisation of a recipe from my uncle Tim's restaurant, Juveniles, in Paris where they have served the cake – using the dark, delicious Valrhona chocolate – for over 10 years. It is supposed to be moist inside, that's what's so good about it. We make it at The Atlas using a white chocolate from Venezuela called El Rey.

200g/7oz white chocolate, chopped
200g/7oz unsalted butter, chopped
250g/9oz almond flour, sifted

200g/7oz caster sugar
8 eggs
150g/5oz blackberries

For the Mascarpone Cream
250g/9oz mascarpone
2 egg yolks
75g/3oz caster sugar

First, turn on the oven to 170°C/325°F/gas 3. There is nothing worse than having a cake mixture sitting about waiting for the oven to warm up. Melt the chocolate and butter together in a bowl over a saucepan of hot water. Add the almond flour and sugar and mix in with a whisk. The mixture will be quite thick and stodgy. Add all the eggs and continue to whisk in gently. When everything is combined, add the blackberries and stir one last time. Pour into a buttered and floured 25cm/10" cake tin and bake for 10 minutes. Leave the cake to cool slightly before inverting on to a wire rack to cool completely.

To make the mascarpone cream, scrape the mascarpone into a mixing bowl. Using a wooden spoon, gently beat in the egg yolks and sugar. You may think that the mixture will never loosen, but persevere and the result will be a bright yellow, creamy texture. Serve with the cake.

Serves 8

And... | 'Bruschetta di Ricotta' with Sautéed Spinach and Marinated Grapes

This dish, quite literally, came together rather by default on a Sunday night at the Fox and Hounds when we were faced with a blank space on the menu and only these ingredients left in the 'cupboard'. Aim for top quality ricotta, the cheap stuff is so bland it doesn't really complement the dish.

For the Marinade
100ml/3^1/2fl oz extra virgin olive oil, plus extra for drizzling and cooking
50ml/2fl oz balsamic vinegar
^{1}/2 bunch of flat leaf parsley, coarsely chopped

salt and pepper

200g/7oz seedless white and red grapes, sliced
^{1}/2 red onion, finely diced
4 slices of hearty country bread
1 garlic clove, sliced

leaves from 300g/10oz spinach, washed and dried
250g/9oz ricotta
50g/2oz pine kernels, lightly toasted

Begin by making a marinade for the grapes. Combine the olive oil, balsamic vinegar, parsley, a pinch of salt and plenty of cracked black pepper in a measuring jug or similar container. Hold the whisk between the palms of both hands and rotate furiously as if you are trying to make fire from two pieces of wood. An opaque emulsion should form pretty quickly. Pour over the grapes and red onion and leave to marinate for at least 20 minutes.

Toast the bread, rub with the garlic clove, drizzle with olive oil and keep warm.

Place a wok over a medium heat and pour in a good splosh of olive oil. This is the final stage, everything else must be ready because spinach, once cooked, must be eaten immediately, before it wilts into compost, reminiscent of Sunday lunches at my grandparents' house. As soon as the oil is hot, throw in the garlic and quickly follow with the spinach. If the spinach is not thoroughly dry, you'll end up with a wok full of soggy greens and ditch water. As soon as the leaves are beginning to wilt remove them and place an amount on top of each slice of toasted bread.

'Crumble' the ricotta using two spoons (not fingers – it won't go where you want it to – like window putty, it just spreads across your hand) to arrange little blobs along the top of the spinach. Spoon on the grapes and dressing and sprinkle on the pine kernels. Serve immediately.

Serves 6

And...   Celeriac and Beetroot Soup with Chilli, Paprika and Ginger

Ed, who now heads the kitchen at the Fox and Hounds, experimented for weeks with beetroot to see how many different things we could make with this affordable and readily available veg. This was one of the best discoveries, sweet and spicey, and now a regular fixture on the Atlas menu.

olive oil, for cooking
knobs of butter, for cooking
1 white onion, chopped
1 leek, chopped
1 celery stick, chopped
1 garlic clove, chopped

1 knob of ginger, chopped
1 red chilli, deseeded and
  chopped
1 tsp paprika
1 small celeriac bulb, chopped
3 small beetroots, boiled &

peeled
about 1l/1^{3}/$_{4}$pt vegetable stock
salt and pepper
soured cream, to serve (optional)

Cover the base of a saucepan with a layer of olive oil and add a knob of butter. Fry the onion, leek, celery, ginger, garlic and chilli until translucent and sweet. Stir the paprika into the vegetables, then add the celeriac. Toss with the other ingredients and add the beetroot.

Cover with vegetable stock and allow to simmer for about 35 minutes. Test with a knife to see if the celeriac is tender. If so, remove from the heat and whizz with a hand-held mixer. We find the hand-held variety better for soups than a food processor simply because you can whizz the soup all in one go rather than in batches, thus controlling the consistency and seasoning more accurately. When you think you've whizzed enough, whizz some more until silky smooth. Add a little stock if too thick.

To finish, add a couple of knobs of butter and season to taste. You can/should serve this with a dollop of soured cream.

Serves 6

BURTS HOTEL
Melrose, Scottish Borders

The Henderson family have been in residence at Burts Hotel for many years and have built up an impressive collection of awards from the food guides. Standing in the charming Market Square of this pretty Borders' village the kitchens produce food that reflects the sporting heritage of the area. Game, seafood and local salmon are mainstays of the kitchen's repertoire. As well as a very good wine list and well kept ales, the bar has a fantastic selection of over 80 malt whiskies.

Starter	Carpaccio of Beef

For the Marinade
450g/1lb coarse salt
225g/8oz brown sugar
zest of 2 lemons
zest of 2 oranges
50g/2oz green peppercorns
25g/1oz cracked black pepper

50g/2oz mixed herbs, chopped
550ml/1pt extra virgin olive oil

For the Beef
1kg/2lb fillet of beef
2 tbsp French mustard
25g/1oz mixed herbs, chopped

150ml/5fl oz extra virgin olive oil
25g/1oz basil
25g/1oz spinach
1 garlic clove
115g/4oz piece of Parmesan

To make the marinade, mix all the ingredients together in a bowl. Unroll a piece of Clingfilm 8 times the length of the beef. Spread some of the marinade on to the Clingfilm covering an area the size of the beef. Place the beef on the marinade and spread with the remaining marinade. Wrap tightly in the Clingfilm and leave in the fridge for at least 48 hours.

Wash off the marinade. Spread over the French mustard and press the herbs on to the mustard. Freeze for 24 hours.

Mix the olive oil, basil, spinach and garlic in a food processor and then pass through a sieve. Slice the thawed beef very thinly, preferably on a gravity slicer. Arrange the slices on a plate – they will defrost in minutes. Using a vegetable peeler, shave flakes of the Parmesan over the beef, and then drizzle with the flavoured oil from the marinade.

Serves 8

Main	Roast Cod

8 x 175g/6oz thick cod fillets
8 slices Parma ham
1 courgette, thinly sliced
  lengthways
2 red peppers, cut into squares
1 aubergine, sliced into rounds
1 red onion, sliced into rounds

1 beef tomato, sliced into
  rounds
oil, for cooking

For the Sauce
300ml/$\frac{1}{2}$ pt double cream
225g/8oz cold butter, diced

25g/1oz basil
2 garlic cloves, chopped
50g/2oz Parmesan, grated
50g/2oz pinenuts, toasted
150ml/5fl oz extra virgin olive oil

Wrap the cod in the Parma ham and set aside.

Dip all the vegetables into oil. Heat a char-grill pan then cook the vegetables in batches until browned and tender. Keep warm. Roast the cod in a preheated oven at 230°C/450°F/gas 8 for 8-10 minutes.

Meanwhile, make the beurre blanc: boil the cream then remove from the heat and gradually whisk in the butter using a hand-held blender. Mix the remaining ingredients together in a food processor then add to the beurre blanc.

Divide the char-grilled vegetables among 8 plates and put the cod on top. Spoon the sauce around the fish.

Serves 8

Dessert | Iced Glayva with Raspberries

115g/4oz sugar	115ml/4oz oatmeal, toasted	**For the Glayva Syrup**
8 eggs, separated	40ml/1$\frac{1}{2}$fl oz Glayva liqueur	2 tbsp honey
300ml/$\frac{1}{2}$pt double cream	115g/4oz raspberries	100g/3$\frac{1}{2}$oz poppy seeds
2 tbsp honey	sprigs of mint, for garnish	40ml/1$\frac{1}{2}$fl oz Glayva liqueur

Whisk the sugar and egg yolks until white and the whisk leaves a trail when lifted. Bring the cream to the boil then stir into the sugar and eggs. Return to the pan and cook over a very low heat, stirring all the time with a wooden spoon, until the sauce is thick enough to cover the back of the spoon. Do not allow to boil. Cover the surface of the sauce with Clingfilm and leave to cool.

Whisk the egg whites until stiff and fold into the cold sauce with the honey, oatmeal and Glayva. Pour into a freezer-proof dish lined with Clingfilm and put in the freezer until firm, or churn in an ice-cream maker.

To make the syrup, mix the honey and Glayva together then add poppy seeds.

To serve, put the raspberries in the centre of 8 plates. Place a slice of the iced parfait on top and spoon the Glayva syrup around. Garnish with fresh sprigs of mint.

Serves 8

And... | Pink Grapefruit Marmalade

6 pink grapefruit	300ml/$\frac{1}{2}$pt white wine vinegar
450g/1lb brown sugar	1 red onion, finely sliced

Peel the grapefruit with a vegetable peeler and shred the skin very finely. Put the skin, sugar, vinegar and onion into a pan (not aluminium), and boil until thick and syrupy. Divide the grapefruit into segments and add to the syrup. Leave to cool. Store in the fridge, where it can be kept for a long time.

Makes 450g/1lb

And... | Parmesan Wafers

450g/1lb fresh Parmesan, finely grated

Use the cheese to make 16 mounds about 15cm/6" in diameter, on greaseproof-paper-lined baking sheet(s). Bake in batches in a preheated oven at 220°C/425°F/gas 7 for 10 minutes until golden brown. Leave to cool slightly before carefully removing from the paper.

Makes 16

THE CHOLMONDELEY ARMS
Cholmondeley, Cheshire

The inn stands adjacent to the grounds of Cholmondeley Castle and was the village schoolhouse until 1982 when it was bought by Guy and Carolyn Ross-Lowe, who then turned it into one of the best food pubs in Britain. Its previous life as a schoolhouse enabled the Ross-Lowes to make use of some unusual architectural features and create a relaxed and individual setting for their splendid food.

Starter — Home-potted Shrimps

75g/3oz butter
1 tsp freshly ground black
  pepper
1 tsp ground mace

good pinch of cayenne pepper,
  to taste
salt
350g/12oz shelled, cooked fresh

shrimps
lemon wedges and hot brown
  toast, to serve

Melt the butter gently and then add the spices and salt. Fold the shrimps into the butter but do not cook. Press gently into 4 ramekins and leave to cool before putting in the fridge.

To serve, take out of the fridge at least 30 minutes before you plan to eat. All they need is a wedge of lemon and hot brown toast to accompany them.

Serves 4

Main — Braised Tongue with Shrewsbury Sauce

1 whole pickled tongue, soaked
  overnight in clean water
50g/2oz streaky bacon,
  chopped
2 carrots, chopped
2 small onions, chopped
3 celery sticks, chopped

50g/2oz butter
50g/2oz flour
550ml/1pt red wine
2 tsp tomato purée
2 tbsp redcurrant jelly

For the Garlic Mash
1kg/2lb potatoes, chopped
4-6 garlic cloves
salt and pepper
50g/2oz butter, melted
110ml/4floz double cream
dribble of extra virgin olive oil

Drain the tongue and put in a pan of fresh cold water to cover. Bring slowly to the boil and then simmer for about 2½ hours. Leave to cool in the water before removing skin and trimming the back of the tongue, making sure there are no bones. Reserve the cooking liquid.

In a heavy-based casserole pan, cook the bacon, carrots, onions and celery in the butter until soft. Place the tongue on the top of the vegetables and add enough of the reserved liquid to come half way up the tongue. (If the liquid is very salty replace with half water.) Cover with foil and a tight-fitting lid and braise in a preheated oven at 180°C/350°F/gas 4 for about 1 hour. Remove the tongue and keep warm. Strain the juice from the vegetables and reserve. Add the flour to the vegetables and mix well. Cook until just beginning to brown.

Make up the reserved cooking liquid to 1.1¹/₂ pt and add the red wine, tomato purée and redcurrant jelly. Simmer, stirring, until it becomes a coating consistency and then strain.

Meanwhile, make the garlic mash: boil the potatoes until almost cooked then throw in the garlic. When the potatoes are cooked, drain well and, using either a hand whisk or an electric whisk, beat until fluffy adding salt and pepper, the melted butter and the cream. A dribble of extra virgin oil makes it even richer.

Slice the tongue into 2cm/³/₄" slices and coat with the redcurrant Shrewsbury sauce. Serve with the garlic mash.

Serves 4-6

Dessert | Summer Fruit Brûlée

Any fruit will do but a mixture of raspberries, strawberries, nectarines and blueberries is a good combination. Slice the nectarines leaving the skin on and halve or quarter the strawberries
Cointreau, Grand Marnier or the liqueur of your choice, for sprinkling

175ml/6fl oz whipping cream
175ml/6fl oz crème fraîche
demerara sugar

Gently mix all the fruit together and divide among 4 ramekins, or put into one large dish to just half fill it. Sprinkle with a little Cointreau, Grand Marnier or other liqueur.

Whip the cream to soft peaks and then fold in the crème fraîche. Spoon over the fruit and smooth the tops. Chill until really cold.

Preheat the grill until very, very hot. Sprinkle demerara sugar thickly over the cream mixture. Place as close to the grill as possible until the sugar caramelises. Allow to cool before serving.

Serves 4

And... | Hot Cherry Tomato Crostini

450g/1lb cherry tomatoes, halved
50ml/2floz olive oil, plus extra for brushing
2 garlic cloves, crushed
25g/1oz caster sugar
salt and pepper
8 x 2cm/³/₄" slices of French bread
balsamic vinegar, for sprinkling
1 packet buffalo mozzarella, cut into thin slices
basil, for garnish

Put the tomatoes on a baking tray. Mix the olive oil, garlic and sugar together and pour over the tomatoes. Sprinkle with salt and pepper. Bake in a preheated oven at 220°C/425°F/gas 7 for about 20 minutes.

Meanwhile, brush the slices of French bread with a little olive oil and bake in the oven for about 10 minutes until just crunchy.

Sprinkle the tomatoes with balsamic vinegar and pile on to the toasted bread. Cover each one with a slice of mozzarella. Put under a preheated grill until the top has melted, then garnish with plenty of basil.

Serves 4

And...	**Crab Apple and Mint Jelly**

equal quantities of eating apples   sugar   mint
 and crab apples, chopped   lemons

Put the apples and crab apples in a non-aluminium pan, cover with water and bring to the boil. Simmer for about 1¼ hours until the crab apples are pulpy. Pour the apple mixture into a jelly bag, or use a double thickness of cheesecloth or muslin, suspended over a bowl, and leave to drip overnight; do not push the fruit or squeeze the bag because this will make the jelly cloudy.

Measure the juice into a clean pan and stir in 450g/1lb sugar for every 550ml/1pt juice. Add the juice of 2 lemons for every 6.8l/12pt of juice. Heat gently, stirring, until the sugar has dissolved, then increase the heat and boil hard, skimming the surface as necessary, for about 10 minutes until setting point is reached. (To test for setting point, remove the pan from the heat, drop a little of the jelly on to a cold saucer; push it gently with a fingertip and if it wrinkles it is ready.)

Meanwhile, chop 3 good handfuls of mint per 6.8l/12pt juice.

Leave the jelly to cool slightly then stir in the mint. Pour into warm, scrupulously clean, dry jars, cover and seal. Leave overnight to set. Store in a cool, dry, dark place.

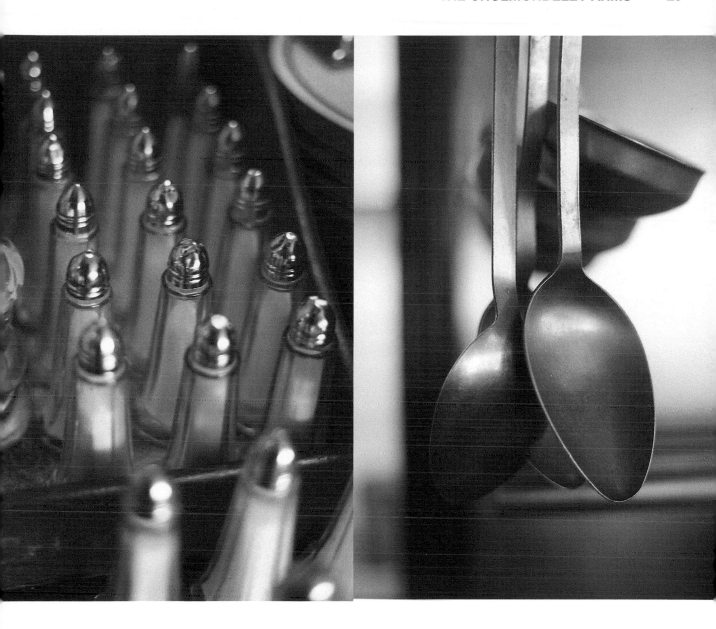

THE COW
Westbourne Park Road, London W2

Tom Conran's fashionable and buzzy pub near Notting Hill does many things very well, but it is fish that is king here. A great bar downstairs and the slightly more formal but still relaxed dining room upstairs serve some of the best seafood to be found in London. Head Chef, James Rix. has a seemingly limitless repertoire of dishes and his kitchen manages to produce meals of the highest quality even when under the severest pressure – and The Cow is a place that can get very busy!

Starter | Grilled Razor Clams with Garlic Butter

Razor clams are very strange looking shellfish but are delicious none the less. They are available from May to October. Ours come from Scotland; you should be able to get them from a good fishmonger.

For the Garlic Butter
225g/8oz good quality unsalted
   butter, softened
2 shallots, finely chopped
6 garlic cloves, minced

juice of 1 lemon
handful of chopped parsley
salt and pepper

For the Razor Clams
6-8 razor clams per person
olive oil, for cooking
salt and pepper
8 halved lemons, to serve

To make the garlic butter, beat the butter with the remaining ingredients. Form into a sausage shape, wrap in Clingfilm and chill until firm.

Bring a large saucepan of salted water to the boil. Plunge in the razor clams then immediately remove from the heat and cool the clams in cold water. The clams will open, allowing you to clean them but they will only be partially cooked. Discard any that do not open. Remove the fish from the shells and cut away the black sack that lies halfway down each clam, using a knife or scissors. Return the clams to their shells and arrange on a large baking tray. Drizzle olive oil over the clams and season them.

Dice the garlic butter and put on the top of the clams. Cook under a preheated hot grill for 4-5 minutes until the butter melts and the clams cook through. Do not overcook otherwise they will become coarse and rubbery. Serve immediately with halved lemons.

Serves 8

Main	**Fillet of Wild Sea Trout with Mash, Spinach and Parsley Sauce**

When wild sea trout becomes available it marks the start of spring and is at its best between March and May. It can be tricky to get hold of as the restaurants usually buy it all. It is possible to buy from Club Chef Direct who deliver it to your door. If you are unable to find any wild sea trout then salmon makes a good alternative for this dish.

For the potatoes
500g potatoes, such as Maris
    Piper or Desirée
150ml/5floz double cream
50g/2oz butter
salt and pepper
nutmeg

For the next part of the dish
oil for cooking
4 x 150g/5oz fillets of sea trout
    or salmon, scaled and
    de-boned
flour for coating
salt & pepper

For the sauce
200ml.7floz fish or chicken stock
1 large handful of chopped flat
    leaf parsley
200ml/7floz double cream

For the rest of the dish
2 lemons
200g/7oz blanched spinach
25g/1oz butter

Peel and dice potatoes and put in a pan of salted water, bring to the boil and simmer until tender. Remove from the heat and drain well. Bring the cream and butter to the boil. Mash the potatoes whilst still hot and add the cream and butter. Season with salt, pepper and nutmeg and keep hot.

Heat up a non-stick frying pan and add a little oil. Lightly flour the fillets of trout or salmon, skin side only and season with salt and pepper. Put the fish in the hot pan, skin side down, then turn the heat down. It will need about 4 minutes each side.

Meanwhile, reduce the fish stock by half, add the cream and reduce this by half again. Season with salt and pepper and some lemon juice.

Using another pan, heat the butter and reheat the spinach gently.

Check on the fish, you will want it to be a little pink inside. Add the parsley to the fish sauce, if you have a hand blender you can blitz this to get a greener colour.

Serve on hot plates with a good spoonful of mash in the middle, spinach on top, then the fish. Pour the parsley sauce around and serve with a wedge of lemon.

Serves 4

Dessert | Raspberry Semifreddo Torte

200g/7oz Digestive biscuits	4 large eggs	raspberries, pureed and sieved
100g/3 1/2 almonds, toasted	250g/9oz caster sugar	1/2l/18floz double cream
150g/5oz butter, melted	500g/18oz fresh or frozen	250g/9oz mixed fresh berries

In a food processor or with the end of a rolling pin, crush the biscuits and almonds until fine. Add the melted butter and bind together to form a pastry like texture. Push this mix into a greased 25cm/10" tart case to form the tart case - try to make it as thin as possible. Put the case into the freezer.

In a large bowl whisk the eggs and sugar then place the bowl over a pan of simmering water and whisk until it doubles in volume and thickens.

Next, whisk the double cream until it peaks and then gently combine the sieved raspberries, cream and egg mix. Fold together until mixed through, trying not to knock too much air out of it.

Remove the tart case from the freezer and pour the mixture in, let it settle then put back into the freezer for 4-6 hours until set. Twenty minutes prior to serving remove from the freezer and leave at room temperature.

Serves 6-8

And... | Roast Langoustines with Aïoli and Sweet Chilli Dipping Sauce

Langoustines are always very popular at The Cow and go particularly well with a cool pint of Guinness.

For the Aïoli
2 egg yolks
2 large garlic cloves, crushed
300-450ml/ 1/2- 3/4pt good
  quality vegetable oil

juice of 1 lemon
salt and pepper

For the Langoustines
oil, for cooking

6-7 langoustines per person
bottled sweet chilli sauce, and
  lemons, to serve

For the aïoli, beat the eggs with the garlic and a little salt until thickened. Start to add the oil in a steady, thin stream, whisking continuously. Then add a little of the lemon juice and more oil and continue until they have both been used up and you have a thick mayonnaise. Season and set aside.

Pour a thin layer of oil into a baking sheet or shallow baking tin that is large enough to hold all the langoustines, put into the oven and preheat to 230°C/450°F/gas 8. When the oil is hot, toss the langoustines into the tin to coat in the oil. Season and return to the oven for 5-6 minutes. Leave to cool slightly before serving with the aïoli and chilli sauce in separate bowls, plus lemons and something to clean your fingers.

Serves 6-8

And...   The Cow Fish Stew

This stew is best made with some shellfish shells, and bones from good, white flatfish such as sole and halibut. You can use the shells from the prawns and buy fish bones from the fishmonger.

2 celery stalks, diced
1 onion, diced
1 fennel bulb, diced
2 carrots, diced
2 red chillies, diced
4 garlic cloves, chopped
1 bay leaf
1/2 bunch of tarragon
1/2 bunch of dill

2 sprigs of thyme
few parsley stalks
oil, for cooking
500g/1lb 2oz can tomatoes
1/2 bottle white wine
500g/1lb 2oz shellfish shells
2kg/4lb white fish bones
salt and pepper
Variety of seafood and fish such

as mussels, prawns, sliced
  squid and diced cod fillet
seasoned flour, as much or as
  little as you like
splash of Pernod
chopped parsley leaves, to
  garnish
bread, to serve

Fry the vegetables and herbs in some oil in a large pan over a brisk heat for about 6-8 minutes, then add the tomatoes and wine. Boil until reduced by half. Add the fish bones and shells, barely cover with water and bring to the boil. Simmer for 45 minutes. Purée in a blender or push through a coarse sieve using the back of a soup ladle. Return to the pan, add the Pernod, bring to the boil then reduce by half. Season and strain through a fine sieve.

Lightly coat the fish pieces in seasoned flour and fry until golden. Add to the stew with the prawns and mussels and simmer for 3-4 minutes until the mussels open. Discard any unopened ones. Serve in a deep bowl with parsley sprinkled over and accompanied by bread.

Serves 6-8

THE CRICKETERS
Clavering, Essex

The Cricketers is very much the creation of Trevor and Sally Oliver. A family concern since 1976, the couple have made this charming 16th-century Essex pub, in the pretty village of Clavering near Saffron Walden, a great place to visit for food of the highest quality served in friendly and attractive surroundings. Trevor Oliver trained as a chef at the legendary A L'Ecu de France in Soho, and his passion for the very best produce cooked to the highest standards sets the tone for this great pub.

Starter	Confit of Duck, with White Haricot Beans, Bacon and Asparagus

6–8 garlic cloves, crushed (keep 1 or 2 cloves for the haricot beans)
pinch of Chinese five spice powder
few sprigs of thyme, bruised (keep a couple of sprigs for the haricot beans)
35g/1^1/2oz sea salt
4 duck legs
250g/9oz haricot beans

4 tbsp olive oil
500g/1lb 2oz duck or goose fat (You can buy duck or goose fat from delicatessens, good butchers and even some supermarkets now.)
3 ripe tomatoes, squashed
salt and pepper
100g/3^1/2oz pancetta or smoked streaky bacon, cut into lardons

1 bunch of asparagus
handful of mixed soft herbs and some mixed leaves (like rocket, baby spinach, baby chard or mizuna), to serve

For the Dressing
3 tbsp olive oil
1 tbsp sherry vinegar or white wine vinegar

Mix the garlic, five spice powder, thyme and salt together and rub really well over the duck legs. Cover with Clingfilm and refrigerate overnight. Soak the haricot beans in water overnight.

The following day, carefully brush or scrape off the seasonings. Heat 2 tablespoons of the oil and fry the duck legs for about 8 minutes until golden brown. Transfer to an ovenproof dish, skin side up. Cover with the duck or goose fat and cook in a preheated oven at 140°C/275°F/gas 1 for about 2^1/2 hours until the meat is nearly falling off the bone. Leave the legs to cool in the fat. Refrigerate, as these can be cooked in advance.

Cook the haricot beans in water until tender (see packet for times) with the remaining thyme and garlic and the tomatoes. Drain and season with salt, pepper and the remaining olive oil.

To make the dressing, whisk the oil and vinegar together with seasoning until emulsified. Fry the lardons until crisp. Cook the asparagus in boiling salted water until still slightly crunchy (al dente). Cut the asparagus into lozenge-sized pieces then mix with the haricot beans and lardons.

Remove most of the fat from the duck legs. Put them into a roasting tin in a preheated oven at 230°C/450°F/gas 8 for about 8-10 minutes, turning them over halfway through. The duck skin should be nice and crisp. To serve, toss the mixed leaves and herbs in the dressing and place on each plate. Divide the haricot bean mixture over them, then place the duck legs on top.

Serves 4

| **Main** | **Calves' Liver on a Mash of Potato and Scallions with Shallot Gravy** |

This is lovely served with some nice green vegetables. You can also use grilled smoked back bacon instead of the sage leaves.

8 shallots, chopped
175g/6oz butter, melted, plus
  extra for frying
2-3 tbsp white wine vinegar
1 tsp sugar
1.4l/2pt good veal or beef stock

salt and pepper
4 large potatoes
175g/6oz butter, melted, plus
  extra for frying
125ml/4$\frac{1}{2}$fl oz double cream
1 bunch of spring onions, very

thinly sliced
4 x 200g/7oz slices calves' liver
oil, for frying
sage leaves (optional)

Cook the shallots in a little butter over a low heat until soft. Add the vinegar and sugar and boil until the pan is nearly dry. Add the stock and reduce by two thirds. Season to taste and keep warm.

Meanwhile, boil the potatoes in salted water until tender. Drain and then mash them. Mix in the melted butter and cream and finally add the spring onions and seasoning.

Fry the liver in hot oil in a very hot pan (a griddle pan is good for this) on both sides until pink in the middle, or to your liking. This will not take very long. Remove and keep warm. If using sage leaves, fry them in the fat until crisp. Serve the liver on top of the mash, with the sauce poured around and the sage leaves scattered over.

Serves 4

Dessert | Lemon Tart with Spiced Tamarillos

zest and juice of 6 lemons
500g/1lb 2oz caster sugar
9 large free-range eggs
400ml/14fl oz double cream
1 pastry case in a 20cm/10" tart
  tin, baked blind and egg
  washed

250g/9oz crème fraîche, to
  serve

For the Spiced Tamarillos
250ml/9fl oz redcurrant jelly
250ml/9fl oz red wine
250ml/9fl oz port

1 cinnamon stick
1 star anise
1 vanilla pod
5 black peppercorns
5 juniper berries (optional)
4 tamarillos

Place the lemon juice and zest into a bowl. Add the caster sugar and mix thoroughly. Next whisk in 3 whole eggs and the yolks of the other 6 eggs, until smooth. Stir in the double cream. Pour into the pastry case and cook in a preheated oven at 110°C/225°F/gas 1/4 for 45 minutes or until set. Leave to cool, then refrigerate before serving.

To make the spiced tamarillos, put the redcurrant jelly, red wine, port, cinnamon stick, star anise, vanilla pod, peppercorns and juniper berries, if using, in a saucepan and bring to the boil. Add the tamarillos and allow to boil until the skin of the tamarillos begins to split. Remove from heat. Pour into a large open dish to cool quickly, then refrigerate.

To serve, cut the tart into 8 slices and simply serve with a spoonful of crème fraîche and half a spiced tamarillo. Drizzle the sauce from the tamarillos around the tart.

Serves 8

And... | Char-grilled Peaches with Mexican Honey and Vanilla Mascarpone

6 firm but ripe peaches
2 tsp olive oil

350g jar Mexican honey
100g/3 1/2 oz caster sugar

seeds from 1 vanilla pod
250g/9oz mascarpone cheese

Cut the peaches around the middle, then twist to remove one half from the stone. Remove the stone from the other half of the peach. Lightly brush the cut sides of the peach with olive oil to prevent them from sticking to the pan during cooking. The peaches should be placed cut side down on the griddle/char grill until they have char marks on them. (Or, this can be done in a frying pan, to lightly colour the peaches.)

Place the peaches in a small roasting tin. Drizzle over the honey and sprinkle with the caster sugar. Bake in a preheated oven at 200°C/400°F/gas 6 for 5-10 minutes, depending on the ripeness of the peaches. When cooked, the peaches should retain their shape but be exceptionally soft.

Add the seeds from the vanilla pod to the mascarpone cheese. Place 3 peach halves on each plate and drizzle over the juices from the roasting tin. Serve with a quenelle of the mascarpone cheese.

Serves 4

And... **Potato and Rosemary Focaccia**

1 x 7g sachet of dried yeast
1oz sugar
425ml/15floz tepid water
500g/1lb strong flour
250g/8oz semolina

15ml/$^1/_2$oz salt
extra flour for dusting
5-7 new potatoes, scrubbed
1 clove of garlic, finely chopped
a few twigs of fresh rosemary,

roughly chopped
freshly ground pepper
extra virgin olive oil
sea salt

Dissolve the yeast and sugar in half the tepid water.

Mix the flour, semolina and salt, make a well in the middle and add the dissolved yeast mixture, stirring in circular movements from the centre outwards until all the yeast mixture is soaked up. Add the rest of the water and mix to make a nice dough. Knead for about 5 minutes until nice and silky. Flour your hands and dust a little over the dough, make it into a roundish shape and place on a tray. Score the dough with a knife. Leave the bread to prove until double in size. It should be proved in a draught-free, warm place and can take between 40 minutes and 1$^1/_2$ hours depending on the temperature and conditions.

During this time heat the oven to 170-180°C/340-350°F/gas 3-4. Slice the new potatoes thinly then boil in salted water for about 2 minutes. Drain them and put into a bowl with the garlic, rosemary and black pepper then mix with a generous amount of extra virgin olive oil.

When the dough has doubled in size, 'knock it back' by kneading again for about a minute and knocking the air out of it.

Dust a large tray (about 30cm x 45cm x 2.5cm/12" x 18" x 1" deep) with flour and roll the dough out to about 1$^1/_2$cm/$^2/_3$" thick, in a shape roughly the size and shape of the tray. Scatter and smear the potato mixture all over the bread, pushing your fingers right into the dough so that the flavours can penetrate into the bread. Leave to prove as before, until it is about 3cm/1" thick.

Bake for 30 minutes, remove from the oven, drizzle with extra virgin olive oil and cover with a scattering of sea salt. Cut into squares and serve warm.

THE CROWN
Grove Road, London E3

The Crown was the second of Esther Boulton's and Geetie Singh's organic pubs (see page 104 for The Pelican and page 38 for The Duke of Cambridge). A wonderful Victorian building, with balconies that overlook Victoria Park, it serves the same high standard of award-winning European influenced dishes as its sister pubs, all using exclusively organic ingredients. The decor is simple and open-plan and the wooden furnishings are delightfully mismatched, a style that is peculiar to the urban 'gastropub' pioneered in London.

Starter	Chicory and Avocado Caesar Salad

For the Caesar Dressing
3 garlic cloves
5-10 anchovy fillets, depending on how strong you like the dressing
2 egg yolks
500ml/18fl oz olive oil
500ml/18fl oz vegetable oil

squeeze of lemon juice
handful of grated Parmesan cheese
pepper

For the Salad
1 loaf, such as a bloomer, crusts removed, cut into 1cm/$^1/_2$"

cubes
olive oil
salt and pepper
1 head of chicory
1 ripe avocado
grated Parmesan cheese, to serve

To make the dressing, in a pestle and mortar or food processor, crush the garlic and anchovy fillets. Add the egg yolks and mix thoroughly. When you have a paste, start adding the oils drop by drop. You should have an emulsion. Keep going until you have used all the oil. (If the sauce becomes very thick at the beginning, thin by adding a few drops of water.) Stir in the lemon juice, Parmesan and black pepper. Set aside. This makes a large quantity of dressing and be kept stored in the fridge in a sealed jar. Halve or quarter if desired.

Spread the bread cubes on a baking tray and drizzle lightly with olive oil and season. Toast in the oven until golden brown and crunchy.

Unravel the chicory leaves and slice in half, if necessary. Add to a large bowl with similar sized slices of avocado. Add the croutons and enough dressing to cover the leaves and avocado. Pile onto a plate and scatter over some more Parmesan.

Salad quantity serves 2

Main | Rib-eye Steak with Béarnaise Sauce, Chips and Spring Greens

Choose nice organic rib-eye steaks. The rib-eyes we use are Welsh and is by far the most popular dish in all our pubs.

6 x about 225g/8oz rib-eye steaks
1 sprig of rosemary, bashed or chopped
4 sprigs of thyme, bashed or chopped
4 large potatoes (do not peel), cut into thick chips

500g/1lb 2oz spring greens, chopped
oil, for deep frying

For the Béarnaise Sauce
1 shallot, chopped
6 peppercorns
2 stalks of tarragon, leaves

reserved
1 bay leaf
100ml/3$\frac{1}{2}$fl oz white wine vinegar
2 egg yolks
250g/9oz butter, chopped
salt and pepper

Scatter the rosemary, thyme and some black pepper over the steaks, cover and leave to marinate until you are ready to cook them.

Cook the chips in boiling salted water until almost tender. Drain well. (Or blanch the chips in a deep-fat fryer on the lowest setting.) Set aside.

Cook the spring greens in boiling salted water for 2 minutes. Drain well and set aside.

To make the sauce, put the shallot, peppercorns, tarragon stalks, the bay leaf and vinegar into a saucepan and boil until the vinegar is reduced to 2 tablespoons. Put the egg yolks into a bowl and strain on the reduced vinegar. Whisk thoroughly. Heat the butter until just boiling. Start slowly ladling the butter on to the egg yolks while whisking all the time. The sauce should then emulsify (do not use the milky layer of butter at the bottom of the saucepan). Finish the sauce with the tarragon leaves, and seasoning. Keep warm over a saucepan of hot water.

Grill or fry the steaks for 6-15 minutes depending on whether you like them to be rare, medium or well done.

Meanwhile, heat a deep pan half-filled with oil to 185°C/360°F. Add the chips in batches and fry for 2-3 minutes until golden and crisp. Drain well.

Toss the greens in oil or butter and season well. Pile the chips and greens separately on to plates, place the steaks on top and pour over a generous amount of the sauce.

Serves 6

Dessert · Biscotti with Dessert Wine

Another great stand by – terrific with coffee or served with chocolate mousse, ice creams, etc.

200g/7oz butter, softened
600g/1lb 5oz icing sugar
4 eggs, beaten
seeds of 2 vanilla pods

scraped out
4 tsp brandy
900g/2lb plain flour
2 tsp bicarbonate of soda

600g/1lb 5oz hand-chopped
almonds or hazelnuts

Cream together the butter and sugar. Add the eggs, vanilla seeds and brandy and then fold in the flour, bicarbonate of soda and nuts. Work until you get dough and then separate into 4 logs. Chill until hard. Place the logs on a baking tray, well spaced out. Bake in a preheated oven at 170-180°C/325-350°F/gas 3-4 for about 30 minutes. They should then feel like a cross between a cake and a biscuit, and no indentation should be left in the dough after you press it. Leave to cool then, using a sharp or serrated knife, cut slices of about 5mm/1/4" thick. Place these on a baking tray and put back into the oven at 170°C/325°F/gas 3 for 1 hour until dry and hard. Once cool, store in an airtight container.

Serve with a glass of organic Saussignac dessert wine and don't be afraid to dunk the biscotti in the wine....

Makes about 15

And... · Spiced Merguez Sausages with Tomato Chilli Jam

For the Merguez
375g/13oz finely minced lamb
225g/8oz finely minced beef
1 garlic clove
1/2 tsp paprika
1/2 tsp caraway
1/2 tsp chilli seasoning

pig's caul (optional)

For the Tomato Chilli Jam
2 x 400g/14oz cans of chopped
  tomatoes
1 chilli, split
1 bay leaf

250g/9oz sugar
seasoning

500g/18oz green beans
fresh mint,olive oil, Little Gem
  lettuce,toasted sesame seeds,
  to serve

To make the merguez, mix all ingredients together and shape into sausages or small burgers. They can be wrapped in pig's caul for extra security. Cook on a barbecue, grill or fry. To make the chilli jam, put the tomatoes in a wide, heavy-bottomed saucepan. Add the chilli and bay leaf and cook for about 15 minutes until the tomatoes begin to break down. Add the sugar and continue cooking until you have a jam-like consistency. Season and leave to cool. Pour into a Kilner jar and refrigerate. Can be used like a relish with meats or cheese.

Top and tail the green beans then cook them in boiling salted water. Refresh in cold water while still crisp. When dry, toss with fresh mint, olive oil, Little Gem and toasted sesame seeds. Serve the merguez with the beans and a big dollop of tomato chilli jam.

Serves 16 as a starter, 8 as a main course

And...   Spinach and Ricotta Gnocchi with Tomato Sauce and Parmesan

This recipe comes from the book *Verdura* by Viana La Place.

For the Tomato Sauce
1 onion, chopped
butter, for cooking
1kg/2lb peeled, seeded and
   chopped tomatoes
large handful basil leaves, ripped

For the Gnocchi
1kg/2lb spinach
3 eggs, beaten
150g/5oz Parmesan cheese,
   grated, plus extra for sprinkling
150g/5oz pecorino cheese,
   grated (or use a total of
   300g/10oz Parmesan
   cheese,only)

500g/18oz ricotta
200g/7oz plain flour, plus extra
   for dusting
grated nutmeg
salt and pepper

grated mozzarella cheese, for
   sprinkling
mixed leaf salad, to serve

To make the sauce, cook the onion in a little butter until soft but not coloured. Add the tomatoes and cook until the tomatoes give off their juices. Stir in the basil and seasoning. Set aside.

Wilt the spinach in batches in a large saucepan. Drain well, leave to cool then squeeze until quite dry. Finely chop the spinach and put in a large bowl with the remaining ingredients except the mozzarella and salad. Mix well and shape into walnut-sized balls. Dust lightly with flour. Bring a large saucepan of salted water to the boil. Add the gnocchi a few at a time; they will rise to the surface when cooked. Remove with a slotted spoon and drain on a clean tea towel.

Toss the gnocchi with the sauce, put in a heatproof dish and sprinkle over Parmesan and mozzarella cheese to cover the top. Put under a preheated grill until the cheese has melted. Serve with a mixed leaf salad.

Serves 4-6

THE DUKE OF CAMBRIDGE
St Peter Street, London N1

This was the first of Esther Boulton's and Geetie Singh's much acclaimed trio of organic pubs in London, the others being The Crown (see page 34) and The Pelican (see page 104). Surrounded by Georgian houses, this Victorian pub has a small, quirky and intimate dining room and a charming outside courtyard. The food here, cooked by Head Chef Caroline Hamlin and her team, is based on the philosophy of producing uncomplicated seasonal dishes and drawing freely on the varied influences of European cooking.

Starter | Swiss Chard and Parmesan Tart

1kg/2lb Swiss chard
2 onions, chopped
4 garlic cloves, chopped
oil, for frying
a few sprigs of thyme, chopped
300ml/$\frac{1}{2}$pt milk
300ml/450g/1lb puff pastry
550ml/1pt double cream
4 eggs, beaten

small handful of grated
Parmesan cheese, plus extra for
  sprinkling
nutmeg
salt and pepper
dressed salad leaves such as
  frisée, rocket, radicchio, Little
  Gem and flat leaf parsley

For the Pastry
500g/1lb 2oz plain flour
250g/9oz butter, diced
1 tbsp olive oil
cold water

Separate the green part of the Swiss chard leaves from the stalks. Cook the stalks in boiling salted water until tender then remove them from the water. Drop the green parts into the same water for 1 minute until wilted. Drain and squeeze dry. Leave to cool with the stalks.

To make the pastry, put the flour and butter into a food processor and mix until they look like breadcrumbs. Add the seasoning, olive oil and enough cold water to form a dough. Wrap in Clingfilm and chill for 20 minutes.

Roll out the dough to fit a loose-bottomed tart tin. Line the tin with the pastry, pushing into the edges but do not stretch it. Bake blind (cover with baking parchment and baking beans) in a preheated oven at 200°C/400°F/gas 6 for about 15 minutes. Remove the beans and baking parchment and cook for a further 5 minutes until the pastry is sandy coloured and crisp. Leave to cool.

Fry the onions and garlic in a little oil over a low heat until soft. Add the thyme sprigs and the chard stalks and greens. Mix with the milk, cream, eggs, and Parmesan. Add a generous grating of nutmeg, and seasoning. Pour into the cooked pastry case and scatter some more Parmesan on top. Bake for about 15 minutes until set. Leave to cool for 10 minutes. Remove from tin, slice and serve with dressed salad leaves.

Serves 8

Main	**Baked Smoked Haddock with Leek Mash and Watercress Sauce**

Pure comfort food for autumn.

2 large potatoes
salt and pepper
2 leeks
butter, for frying
salt and pepper

1 large fillet smoked haddock
  (un-dyed), cut in half

For the Sauce
1 onion
6 cloves

bay leaf
600ml/1pt milk
150g/5oz butter
flour
1 bunch of watercress

Boil the potatoes until tender, then drain well, mash and season. Gently fry the leeks in the butter until soft. Add to the mash with a little milk.

Meanwhile, make the sauce: stud the onion with the cloves and put into a saucepan with the milk, bay leaf and any haddock trimmings. Heat the milk to just on simmering point then leave to infuse for 10 minutes.

In a separate saucepan, melt the butter and stir in the flour to make a sandy paste. Off the heat, slowly ladle the infused milk into the butter and flour, mixing constantly. When all the milk has been added, return the pan to the heat and bring to the boil, stirring. When the sauce has thickened, leave to cook over a very low heat for 5 minutes, stirring occasionally. Strain.

Cook the watercress in boiling water for 4 minutes. Drain and mix with the strained sauce. Pour into a blender and purée to make a vivid green sauce.

Put the haddock on a piece of foil large enough to enclose it, add a small knob of butter, and seasoning. Bake in a preheated oven at 180°C/350°F/gas 4 for 5 minutes or so, depending on thickness. To serve, spoon a pile of the leek mash into deep plates. Place the haddock on top and pour over the watercress sauce.

Serves 2

Dessert — Meringues with Prunes in Armagnac and Praline

A great store cupboard stand by. This recipe is a rough guideline. You can use as much or as little as you like of each ingredient.

For the Prunes in Armagnac
500g/1lb 2oz caster sugar
1 vanilla pod, split
4 shots of Armagnac
500g/1lb 2oz Agen prunes,
    stones removed.

For the Meringue
the quantity of egg white to
    unrefined sugar (eg, 100g egg
    white: 200g sugar)

For the Praline
250g/9oz caster sugar
handful of whole peeled
    almonds or hazelnuts

double cream, to serve

To make the prunes in Armagnac, Place the sugar and vanilla in a pan with 550ml/1pt of water and place on heat to dissolve the sugar. Bring to the boil and cook without stirring until you have a thick syrup. When the syrup is cool, add the Armagnac. Pour over the prunes and marinate in a kilner jar or tightly closed jar for up to 1 month.

Place the egg whites and sugar in the mixing bowl of a food mixer and put over a saucepan of simmering water for about 5 minutes, stirring lightly. Be sure not to let the eggs cook. When all the sugar has dissolved, place bowl on the mixer and whisk at full speed until the mixture is really thick and can hold its own weight in peaks. Spread in small mounds or peaks on a baking tray covered with baking parchment. Cook in the oven on the lowest heat (or leave overnight with the pilot light on) until the meringues are crisp and dry. Store in an airtight container.

To make the praline, put the sugar in a heavy-based saucepan with just enough water to dissolve sugar. Heat gently, stirring occasionally, until the sugar has melted then increase the heat and boil vigorously without stirring until dark golden brown in colour. Spread the almonds or hazelnuts on parchment paper and pour over the syrup. Leave to cool and harden. Smash with a rolling pin.

To serve, whisk the double cream until soft peak stage, then fold in large pieces of broken meringue, prunes cut in half and a sprinkle of praline. Pile onto a plate and drizzle some of the Armagnac syrup over.

Serves 10

And... — Pork Chop with Dijon Mustard

Marinate the pork chops, with some smashed or picked rosemary and black pepper, for 10 minutes. Cut the courgette into rings. Heat olive oil in a frying pan and pan fry the pork chop with rosemary and a sprinkle of salt. When golden brown turn and then add courgettes to the pan. Fry gently until the pork is cooked through. Leave to rest for 5 minutes.

Cook the sugar snap peas in salted boiling water for 1 minute. Toss the sugar snap peas with the courgettes and place on a plate with the pork chop and a large dollop of good quality Dijon mustard. Pour over any juices from the pork.

And...   Chocolate Soufflé Cake

260g/9oz dark chocolate   260g/9oz butter
260g/9oz sugar   9 eggs, separated

Melt the chocolate and butter together over simmering water. Whisk the egg yolks and sugar together until white and doubled in volume. Combine the chocolate and egg mixes together. Whisk the egg whites until stiff, and gently fold into the chocolate mix, one third at a time.

Pour into the loose-bottomed cake tin and cook on 190°C/375°F/gas 5 for approximately 20 minutes or until the cake soufflés slightly but is still wobbly and mousse-like in the middle.

When cooled, serve with crème fraîche and raspberries.

Serves 8-10

THE EAGLE
Farringdon Road, London EC1

Perhaps the phenomenon of the Eagle is best described in the words of Head Chef, Tom Norrington Davies: 'The Eagle story is, by now, something like urban myth, only not made up. Two idealistic chaps took over a dingy old London boozer ten years ago, chucked out the chintz (and the deep-fat fryer) and started a bit of a craze for open-plan, friendly places with decent menus. These places often get called gastropubs by the media, which is a shame, because it rather implies that to be taken seriously, a pub has to become "something else". That certainly wasn't the idea back in 1991 when Mike Belben and David Eyre first threw open the doors at 159, Farringdon Road. Since then The Eagle has become a benchmark for all that's great about real pub food.' Says it all, really.

Starter	White Bean and Rosemary Soup

Cannellini beans are the best option for this soup, which needs no more for a great flavour than fresh rosemary and fruity extra virgin olive oil; buy a good, single estate one and avoid the dreadful blends so often sold in supermarkets. Freshly grated Parmesan also goes well with this soup.

2 sprigs of rosemary	4 tbsp olive oil	sea salt and pepper
salt	2 onions, finely diced	1 mug of extra virgin olive oil
250g/9oz canellini beans, soaked overnight in cold water	2 garlic cloves, chopped	chunks of bread, to serve
	1 tbsp tomato purée	

Here is the fun part. Remove the rosemary leaves from the stalks; keep the stalks to one side. If you have a large pestle and mortar you simply crush the rosemary. If you do not have these items, your largest chopping board and the end of a rolling pin will do the trick. Be as much of a brute to the rosemary as the board (and your kitchen surface!) will allow. Add a little salt to entice juices from the herb, then infuse that with the extra virgin olive oil. Keep to one side.

Note that there is no stock for this soup; the beans will make it for you. To start the beans, drain them from the water they were soaked in and bring them to the boil in a large pan. Cook like this for about 10 minutes, removing any foam that appears on the surface of the water. Then drain them completely.

Now start to cook them again, in about 1.5l/2½pt water. Throw in the rosemary stalks. As soon as the water comes to the boil lower the heat to a slow simmer. The beans will take between 1 and 2 hours. After 1 hour check for tenderness. Whatever you do, never salt dried pulses while you are cooking them as it causes toughness.

Heat the 4 tablespoons of oil in a separate pan. Add the onions and garlic and cook over a low heat for at least 30 minutes; do not let them brown.

When the beans are tender remove them from the heat. Using a potato masher, gently mash the soup until about a third of the beans look smashed up; this will cream the soup a little for you. Add the onions and garlic, and the tomato purée. Return to the heat and cook for another 20 minutes or so. Then season with salt and pepper.

To serve, drizzle as much of the rosemary oil as you wish into the soup. Or serve it on the side with chunks of bread.

Serves 4-6

Main	Tuna with a Sicilian Potato Salad

There must be a book waiting to be written on how one could spend a lifetime eating spectacular variations on a plateful of fish and spuds. A friend from Palermo taught me this way with potatoes but, like many dishes from the southern Mediterranean, it has its roots in North Africa. Be careful to buy good, fresh tuna. Not frozen. (You could use another robust fish such as marlin or swordfish.) Hunt out a 'waxy' variety of potato (the kind with firm yellow flesh). Cyprus or Spunta are the best.

1kg/2lb waxy potatoes, cut into
  rough chunks
400g/14oz can peeled plum
  tomatoes
6-8 tbsp extra virgin olive oil
2 garlic cloves, thinly sliced

2 red onions, thinly sliced
juice of 1 lemon
1 tsp sugar
sea salt and crushed dried
  chillies
4 x 150g/5oz tuna steaks, about

1.5 cm/$^{1}/_{2}$" thick
generous bunch of flat leaf
  parsley

Make the salad just ahead of cooking the fish. You can enjoy the whole ensemble warm or at room temperature but do not chill it. Boil the potatoes first, in plenty of salted water, for 15-20 minutes until they are tender but still hold their shape. Drain and set aside.

Strain the canned tomatoes. Their inclusion in a potato salad may seem odd but here they really do work better than raw, fresh ones. Get your hand into the colander and really squish them to pieces, getting rid of all the juice.

Gently heat half the oil in a thick-bottomed pan. Fry the garlic until translucent, then add the onions, just for a minute or two until they have wilted. Add the tomatoes, lemon juice and sugar. Remove from the heat and pour over the potatoes with the remaining oil. Mix all the ingredients together gently and season with salt and dried chillies. This salad can be as hot or as mild as you wish.

To cook the tuna Eagle-style, heat a griddle pan or heavy-bottomed frying pan over a high heat. Season the tuna with oil and a little salt and add to the pan when it is smoking hot. Sear for just under 1 minute on each side then let it rest for another minute or so off the heat. This will leave the tuna medium-rare which is the best (and possibly the only) way it should be eaten.

Garnish the whole dish with the roughly chopped parsley and perhaps a little more oil.

Serves 4

Dessert   Pasteis de Nata

The overtly pubby atmosphere at the Eagle always meant that we never sold a great deal of desserts. So we ended up with just the one. A Portuguese classic that can be demolished in a couple of mouthfuls. Pasteis de Nata means 'cream tart' although the filling is really a confectioner's custard. Sometimes the tarts are called pasteis de Belem, a reference to the district of Lisbon that is their origin. Go there and you will find places devoted to making these tarts. Lately they have become a regular fixture in many of London's coffee shops. Good news: for they are addictive. Like most Portuguese people we do not make our own. Ours come from a great pâtissier on the South Bank where we also get fantastic Portuguese bread and buns. Should you wish to have a go it is quite fun, and here is a good recipe. The tarts will, however, not look like the shop versions, which are made in the dark of night, under almost tantric secrecy. You can make your own pastry or buy puff pastry ready-made. I generally find ready-made to be excellent.

4 egg yolks	150ml/5fl oz single cream	450g/1lb puff pastry
75g/3oz caster sugar		

To make the custard, cream the egg yolks and sugar until pale and thick. Then gently fold in the cream..

Roll the pastry out until it is about 5mm/¼" thick. Then, along the width of the sheet, turn it into a long Swiss roll shape. Cut cross sections from this, each about 2cm/¾". Press each piece, cut side up, gently into the sections of a muffin tray. You will have strange little tart shells with a curly whirly sort of pattern. Add a little of the cream mix to each shell; do not over fill them.

Bake in a preheated oven at 200°C/400°F/gas 6 for 10-15 minutes. Leave to cool for a short time, these are lovely when eaten warm.

Makes 12-16

THE EAGLE AND CHILD
Bispham Green, Lancashire

In Bispham Green, close to a pretty bowling green, The Eagle and Child is renowned for its straightforward respect of ingredients and dedication to the basic principles of good food – the highest quality produce treated with skill and passion and served in relaxed and friendly surroundings. The owner's family farm the surrounding area and often provide meat, well hung and full of flavour.

Starter | Eagle and Child Hot Smokies

olive oil, for cooking
150g/5oz smoked bacon
  lardons
150g/5oz smoked salmon

trimmings
2 smoked trout fillets
300g/10oz smoked haddock
50ml/2fl oz white wine

400ml/14fl oz double cream
salt and pepper
warm ciabatta, to serve

Warm a little olive oil in a thick-bottomed pan, add the bacon and when this is cooked add the 3 types of fish. Slowly stir until the fish has flaked and is warm and then add the white wine. Reduce by half and add the cream. Bring to the boil and simmer until the cream thickens. Add seasoning and serve with warm ciabatta bread.

Serves 4

Main | Eagle and Child Lamb Steaks with Vegetable Stew

4 x 450g/1lb shoulder steaks,
  including bone
vegetable oil, for cooking
3 large carrots, cut into large

dice
2 onions, cut into large dice
3 garlic cloves, chopped
500g/18oz peeled potatoes, cut

into large dice
1 large leek, cut into large dice
chicken or lamb stock
salt and pepper

Seal the lamb in the vegetable oil in a frying pan then put into a large casserole or a roasting tin. Add the vegetables and enough stock to cover. Seal the casserole or tin with foil and place in a preheated oven at 180°C/350°F/gas 4 for 1-1½ hours.

Remove the meat from the oven, correct the seasoning and serve the meat on top of vegetables.

Serves 4

Dessert — Eagle and Child Raspberry Brûlée

200g/7oz raspberries
115g/4oz caster sugar
cold water

350ml/12fl oz double cream
4 egg yolks
1 split vanilla pod

shortbread biscuits, to serve

Heat the raspberries with 50g/2oz sugar and a little water until the sugar dissolves. Divide the raspberries among 4 ramekins.

Whisk the cream, egg yolks, remaining sugar and the vanilla pod together then pour into the ramekins. Place in a deep tin with 2.5cm/1" of water and bake in a preheated oven at 150°C/300°F/gas 2 until firm. Remove the ramekins from the tin, leave to cool then chill them. Sprinkle with icing sugar and put under a very hot grill until melted. Leave to cool to allow top to set hard. Serve with shortbread biscuits.

Serve 4

And... — Eagle and Child Walnut Bread

1.1kg/2$\frac{1}{2}$lb strong white flour
450g/1lb wholemeal flour
40g/1$\frac{1}{2}$oz salt

300g/10oz chopped walnuts
115g/4oz butter, softened
150g/5oz fresh yeast

50g/2oz caster sugar
850ml/1$\frac{1}{2}$pt warm water

Mix the flours, salt, walnuts and butter in a bowl. In a separate bowl, mix the yeast and sugar into warm water until dissolved. Add to the flour mix and stir together. Leave in the bowl and cover it with a cloth. Leave to prove until doubled in size.

Remove from the bowl, knock down the dough and divide into the size of loaves required. Form into the desired shapes, put on oiled baking sheets and leave to rise again until puffy.

Bake the loaves in a preheated oven 400°C/400°F/gas 6 until brown and the bottom sounds hollow when tapped. Remove from the oven and cool on a wire rack for 30 minutes.

And... — Eagle and Child Apricot Honey

250ml/9fl oz white wine vinegar
225g/8oz demerara sugar

1kg/2lb dried apricots, diced
$\frac{1}{2}$ onion, diced

50g/2oz root ginger, diced
75g/3oz raisins

Boil the vinegar and demerara sugar in a thick-bottomed pan until reduced by half. Add the apricots, onion, ginger and raisins. Top up with water, bring to the boil and simmer for 1$\frac{1}{2}$ hours until thickened. Leave the chutney to cool before serving. Store the chutney in a kilner jar. It will keep for up to 3 months unopened.

THE EAGLE AND CHILD
Stow on the Wold, Gloucestershire

Dating back to 947AD, The Eagle and Child, or at least the building in which it is housed, has been verified as the oldest inn in England by the Guinness Book of Records. Right in the heart of the beautiful Cotswold town of Stow-on-the-Wold, The Eagle and Child is attached to the Royalist Hotel, both owned by former London restaurateurs Alun and Georgina Thomson. Since acquiring the hotel and pub, and then carrying out extensive refurbishments, the food here has received rave reviews and attracted hungry and discerning food lovers from all over.

Starter	Shallot Tatin

400g/14oz round shallots
1kg/2lb duck fat
2 garlic cloves, chopped
4 sprigs of thyme
400g/14oz caster sugar

4 pinches of cracked black
  pepper
115ml/4fl oz white wine
4 discs puff pastry 10cm/4" in
  diameter

4 slices of soft goats' cheese
salad leaves (rocket is ideal as it
  cuts through the sweetness of
  the tatin), to serve

Cook the shallots gently in duck fat. Add the garlic and thyme and continue to cook until soft in the oven at 150°C/300°F/gas 2 for 1-2 hours.

Put the sugar in a heavy saucepan and heat gently until golden brown. Remove from the heat immediately, add the black pepper and carefully pour in the white wine – take care as it might spit. Pour into 4 small tatin pans 10cm/4" in diameter. If you cannot find individual tatin pans, you can make a large tatin using a large pan or ovenproof dish.

Drain and dry the shallots and then place them in the tatin moulds. (Reserve the duck fat and keep in the fridge for making wonderful roast potatoes). Put the pastry on top. Bake in an oven preheated to 200°C/400°F/gas 6 for 15 minutes. Turn on to warmed plates and top with goats' cheese. Garnish with salad leaves.

Serves 4

Main Gloucester Old Spot with Mustard Mash

This is a wonderful winter dish with fantastic flavours and combinations of ingredients. I serve it with mashed potatoes and apple purée, or mashed potatoes flavoured with wholegrain mustard or even a few drops of truffle oil.

1.1kg/2¼lb lean belly of pork, with the fat scored
100g/3½oz butter
2 onions, cut into large dice
2 apples, peeled and quartered

5 sprigs of thyme
6 garlic cloves, crushed
1.1l/2pt cider
500ml/18fl oz chicken stock
500ml/18fl oz veal stock

salt and pepper
mashed potatoes and apple purée, or mashed potatoes with wholegrain mustard, to serve

Cook the pork in the butter in a large, heavy-bottomed saucepan or flameproof casserole until it is turning very rich brown. Remove the meat and add the onions. Fry until browned. Remove and strain the fat from the pan.

Return the meat and vegetables to the pan. Add the apples, garlic, thyme, cider and stocks. Bring to the boil. Season, cover and cook gently in a preheated oven at 180°C/350°F/gas 4 for 4 hours.

Serves 4

Dessert Burnt Lemon Curds

350ml/12fl oz double cream
grated zest and juice of 7 lemons

375g/13oz sugar, plus extra for sprinkling

9 eggs yolks
shortbread, to serve

Warm the cream with the lemon zest and juice in a pan and bring to the boil. Remove from the heat and leave to infuse.

Mix the sugar and yolks and stir in the warm cream mixture. Pour back into the pan, return to the heat and bring to the boil. Strain into 4 ramekins. Leave to cool and then chill.

Sprinkle the tops with sugar and then glaze with a blow torch or place under a preheated, very hot, grill for 5 minutes. Serve with shortbread.

Serves 4

And... Aubergine Caviar

4 aubergines	4 garlic cloves	salt and pepper
4 tbsp good quality olive oil	2 tbsp parsley, chopped	lemon juice, to taste

Brush the aubergines with a little of the oil and bake in a preheated oven at 190°C/375°F/gas 5 for 40-60 minutes until soft. After 20 minutes add the garlic cloves. Leave the aubergines and garlic to cool then peel the aubergines. Put the flesh into a cloth and squeeze dry.

Peel the garlic and put into a food processor with the aubergine flesh, parsley, salt and pepper. Purée until smooth. Gradually beat in the remaining olive oil. When the mixture is stiff stir in the lemon juice. Chill for 2 hours before serving.

Serves 8

And... Ginger Soy Dressing

25g/1oz garlic cloves, chopped	200g/7oz shallots, chopped	150ml/5floz olive oil
50g/2oz ginger, chopped	50ml/2fl oz dark soy sauce	150ml/5floz vegetable oil

Combine all the ingredients. Leave to marinate for at least 1 day before using.

THE FOX
Paul Street, London EC2

The Fox in Paul Street boasts close kinship with the legendary Eagle in Farringdon Road (see page 42), just a 20 minute walk away through the streets of Shoreditch. The Eagle was Michael Belben's and David Eyre's realisation of everything that they wanted from a pub – great food drawing on the influences of southern, Iberian Europe in a completely unstructured pub context. The Fox is Michael's new passion and it is best expressed in his own words: "At the time of writing [2001], the Fox is still a cub. Trish and Harry are assembling our kitchen from a space that was geared to deep fried scampi and the like and are doing a sterling job. We're moving away from our sister pub the Eagle's Iberian slant and heading for who knows where! We want to call our style 'pub dining room', unfussy, good European food." That sounds good to all who know and love the Fox's sister and who are enjoying see her sibling make her own way in the culinary pub world.

Starter	Braised Artichokes with Aïoli

Although cleaning all these artichokes seems quite daunting, it is a fairly simple task, and well worth the end results. Raw artichokes leave a metallic taint on your hands and the knife. Feel free to use gloves and afterwards scrub your knife thoroughly. Any artichokes left over can be chopped through a salad or pasta.

12 baby artichokes, on the stem
juice of 1 lemon
2 lemons, halved
$^1/_2$ onion, diced
1 carrot, diced
1 celery stalk, diced
2 garlic cloves, quite thinly sliced
150ml/5fl oz white wine

100ml/3$^1/_2$fl oz olive oil
1 bay leaf
2-3 sprigs of thyme
salt and peppercorns

For the Aïoli
2 garlic cloves
2 egg yolks

1$^1/_2$ tsp Dijon mustard
salt and pepper
250ml/9fl oz olive oil
lemon juice
small pinch of saffron (optional)

To prepare the artichokes you'll need a large bowl of water with the lemon juice added. Pare back the hardest outer artichoke leaves, about 2 layers, until you get to the pale and tender bottom. Cut the top off, about half way down, just above the hairy choke bit and rub with the cut lemon halves. Then cut the stalk at around 1cm/$^1/_2$" from the base, peel off the outer layer and again rub with the lemon. Throw into the acidulated water. Repeat with the rest of the artichokes.

Put the onion, carrot, celery and garlic into a stainless steel pan, together with the artichokes, wine, olive oil and herbs. Add some salt and a few whole peppercorns. It is preferable to use a wide-based pan so that the artichokes are in one layer and will cook evenly. Add enough water to just cover, and a couple of the lemon halves. Fit over a sheet of greaseproof paper and hold down with a plate to keep the artichokes submerged. Bring to the boil, turn down the heat and simmer for 10-15 minutes, depending on the size. Take off the heat and leave to cool in the liquor. They will now keep for a few days, covered by their liquid, in the fridge.

To make the aïoli, using a mortar and pestle, or a food processor, blend the garlic, egg yolks, mustard, salt and pepper. Slowly work in the oil, as if making mayonnaise, to make a thick sauce.

Season with lemon juice to taste. Stir in the saffron (if using). Leave for a while to let the flavours develop.

Serves 6

Main — Lamb's Sweetbreads, Peas and Tarragon

This dish heralds the arrival of spring; new season's sweetbreads and the first peas of the year. We also like to have the first Jersey Royal potatoes to go either alongside or sauteed with the breads. Feel free to substitute broad beans for the peas, or use a mixture of the two. Mint also works wonderfully.

750g/1$\frac{1}{2}$lb lambs' sweetbreads
sherry vinegar
1-2 bay leaves

salt and pepper
400ml/14fl oz lamb or chicken stock
500g/1lb peas in the pod,

15 tarragon leaves, or a small sprig of tarragon
50g/2oz butter

For the sweetbreads: wash thoroughly under running cold water until the water runs clear. An hour or so would be ideal.

Put the sweetbreads in a saucepan, cover with cold water, add about 1 teaspoon sherry vinegar, a bay leaf or two and a pinch of salt and some pepper. Bring to the boil, quite slowly. Simmer for 1 minute then refresh under running cold water. Peel away the solidified fat and membrane, and drain.

Melt 40g/1$\frac{1}{2}$oz butter in a sauté pan and fry the sweetbreads for about 2 minutes on each side until brown. Deglaze the pan with a smallish splash of sherry vinegar. Add the stock and peas and simmer again for 3-4 minutes. Finish by swirling in the remaining butter and the tarragon.

Serves 6

Dessert — Cherry and Almond Tart

This is a really easy and versatile tart. Use whole almonds as opposed to ground almonds which can be rather dry: this way you will retain the essential oils of the almonds. Change the fruit to suit the season. We use cherries, apricots or nectarines in the summer, plums for autumn, and pears or prunes in the winter.

225g/8oz plain flour
50g/2oz caster sugar, plus extra for macerating
115g/4oz fridge-cold unsalted butter, diced
1 egg, beaten

40ml/1$\frac{1}{2}$fl oz cold milk
600g/1$\frac{1}{2}$ lb pitted cherries
Amaretto or kirsch

For the Frangipane
250g/9oz blanched almonds

50g/2oz caster sugar
25g/1oz flour
250g/9oz unsalted butter, chopped
2 eggs, beaten

In a food processor, blend the flour and sugar to mix it up. Add the cubes of butter until just mixed in (you're looking for a breadcrumb texture). Add the egg and, with the machine running, pour in the milk. Stop the machine as soon as the pastry forms a ball, scrape out the dough and cover in Clingfilm. Refrigerate for 1 hour.

Roll out the dough on a lightly floured board and fit into a 20cm/8" tart tin. Return to the fridge to rest for 30 minutes. Prick the pastry case all over with a fork, cover with greaseproof paper and weigh down with dried beans or rice. Bake in a preheated oven at 180°C/350°F/gas 4 for 20 minutes until dry and firm and slightly coloured.

Meanwhile, sprinkle a handful of sugar over the cherries and leave to macerate for 1 hour.

To make the frangipane, using a food processor, whiz the almonds and sugar until fine. Add the flour, butter and eggs. Process for about 1 minute until creamy. Scrape the frangipane into the cooked tart shell. Lightly push in the cherries. Don't skimp as they will shrink a little during the cooking. Bake for 30 minutes, turn down the oven to 160°C/300°F/gas 2 and continue cooking for 45 minutes.

A little sprinkle of Amaretto or Kirsch on to the tart as it comes out of the oven will add a little extra oomph. Leave the tart to cool before serving at room temperature.

Serves 6-8

And... The Ploughman's Rhubarb Chutney

As a child I always associated pubs with flat-capped men drinking frothy beer from tankards and eating a ploughman's. So I was horrified to discover, later in life, the reality of bland, plastic, yellow slabs of cheese and cubed vegetables in a sticky sauce. We wanted to create the kind of ploughman's of childhood dreams: Neal's Yard has done sterling work providing us with excellent cheeses, and we have tried our best making chutneys and pickles with seasonal fruit and vegetables, our latest being this one made from rhubarb from my Mum's allotment.

1kg/2lb rhubarb
grated rind and juice
  of 2 oranges
450g/1lb onions, finely sliced

850ml/1½pt wine or
  malt vinegar
1kg/2lb brown sugar
1 tbsp whole allspice

1 tbsp mustard seeds
1 tbsp peppercorns

Place the rhubarb, orange, onions, vinegar and sugar in a stainless steel pan. Tie the spices in a piece of muslin and pop it in the pot. Put the pan on the stove and cook over a medium heat for about 1½ hours until thick and pulpy. Pour into hot, scrupulously clean jars and cover with vinegar-proof lids. Store in a cool, dark, dry place.

Now see if you can leave the jars for 2 months before opening them. Even after 2 weeks it'll taste pretty good and you will never know how much better it would have been if you had waited.

Makes about 3l/5½pts

And... The Salt Beef Sandwich

Since we opened, Mike has fantasised about salt beef sandwiches. They do make great pub fodder and somehow seem appropriate as we are situated on the edge of the East End. After a fair bit of research and a couple of attempts we have come up with this as our salt beef sandwich: rye and caraway seed bread, thinly sliced, our own brined organic brisket, American mustard and a gherkin.

For the Brine
5l/8½pt water
1kg/2lb coarse sea salt
500g/18oz brown sugar
1 sprig of bay leaves, rosemary and thyme

1 tbsp juniper berries
(If you can get it, 1 tbsp of salt petre will keep the meat pink)

3k/6-7lb brisket (silverside is a good alternative)

2 carrots, halved
1 onion, halved
1 leek, halved
1 stick of celery, halved
1 bay leaf
pepper

To make the brine, bring the ingredients to the boil in the water so that the salt and sugar dissolve, then leave the brine to cool. Once cool add your brisket, weight it down with a plate or something, and leave for a week in the fridge or a cool place. Now your brisket will have taken on the flavours of the brine and be ready for cooking.

Take the meat from the brine and soak it in clean water either overnight, or perhaps from breakfast until late afternoon. This will mellow the harshness of the salt. Then put the meat in a large, wide saucepan with a leek, onion, celery, bay and pepper. Cover it all with water and simmer for about 2½-3 hours depending on the size of the piece of meat. Make sure you cook it slowly and don't boil it hard.

There it is, it may seem like a lot of work but once you have done it you can feed a family for a week either by slowly reheating the meat in its stock or chopping it and mixing it with potatoes and onion for a corned beef hash.

THE FOX AND HOUNDS
Latchmere Road, London SW11

Sister pub to Richard and George Manners' Atlas (see page 14), The Fox and Hounds is a relatively new venture for the brothers. Following the style of its sibling, the food here is Mediterranean in influence with many of the recipes familiar to devotees of the Atlas. Great food served in relaxed and informal surroundings by friendly and knowledgeable staff are the hallmarks at both pubs.

Starter | Quail and Spinach Risotto

Of all the risottos that we serve at the pub, and we do a different one every day, this one is my favourite. Clare, one of The Atlas's chefs (see page 14), served this up for lunch once and we try to emulate it at The Fox and Hounds. She was cagey about the recipe to start with, but with her imminent departure to begin life in New Zealand, we have managed to tease it out of her!

2 quails	2 sprigs of rosemary	2l/4ptl chicken stock, hot
2 white onions, finely diced	2 handfuls of spinach, washed	pinch of nutmeg
1 stick of celery, finely diced	and de-stemmed	1 tbsp Parmesan
1 leek, finely diced	300g/10oz arborio rice	
4 cloves of garlic		

Start by roasting off the quails, rubbed with lemon zest and rosemary, for approximately 15 minutes in the oven, or until done.

While the quails are in the oven, begin frying the onions, celery, leek, rosemary and garlic in some olive oil in a big wide, ideally stainless steel, saucepan/casserole. As they become translucent, transfer one third to another pot and, over a gentle heat, add the spinach. Cook the spinach right down and then whizz all of the contents of this pan in a food processor. Add a nob of butter and a splash of cream. You are aiming for a thick green paste. Reserve.

Add the rice to the remaining vegetables and slowly, ladle by ladle, begin to add the hot stock. Hot stock is the most crucial factor in cooking risotto. As the rice is slowly absorbing the liquid, remove the meat from the roasted quails by hand and reserve. As the rice reaches the 'al dente' stage, spoon in the spinach paste and stir through. Add the quail, stir, a pinch of nutmeg, stir, a knob of butter, stir, a tablespoon of Parmesan, stir, and finally season appropriately with a little salt. This dish requires patience and vigilance – there are no cheats or shortcuts to making a risotto!

Serves 6

Main | Tunisian Lamb and Aubergine Casserole

The sweet yet wonderfully aromatic dishes from North Africa are very much a feature on the menus at both pubs. Yet they do take time to reach their optimum. Allow 3 hours of cooking time, once assembled, for it to do its thing. If you're making it for lunch, you want to start as soon as you've let the dog out.

For the Couscous Salad
250g/8oz dried couscous
hot water, to cover
knob of butter
zest of 1 lemon
mint, finely chopped
salt

For the Lamb
2kg/4lb stewing lamb

(eg shoulder), cut into
5cm/2"dices
100ml/3$\frac{1}{2}$fl oz olive oil
2 white onions
2 celery sticks
2 leeks
2 carrots
3 aubergines, cut into
5cm/2"cubes
2 tins of tomatoes,

very squeezed
1 tbsp ground cumin
1 tbsp ground coriander
1 tbsp ground ginger
1 tbsp ground turmeric
1 bunch of chopped coriander
250g/8oz dried apricots
1 handful of flaked almonds
salt and pepper
2l/3$\frac{1}{2}$pt meat stock

May I assume that you don't have a couscousière, therefore follow these steps. Place 250g/8oz of dried couscous in a salad bowl. Pour over some hot water, just enough to not cover it! Add a knob of butter, cover with clingfilm for 5 minutes. Grate the zest of one lemon, finely chop some mint. Remove the Clingfilm, stir the couscous with a fork until light and fluffy, then add lemon, mint and salt to taste.

Season and brown the pieces of lamb in 100ml/3$\frac{1}{2}$fl oz of olive oil in a large heavy-bottomed casserole. Remove and keep warm. In the same casserole add a little extra olive oil and add the chopped onions, celery, leeks and carrots. How finely you chop them is up to you – chunky for rustic, super-duper diced if you want to be flash. Use a wooden spoon to scrape the gnarly bits off the bottom of the pan.

While the vegetables are cooking, chop the aubergines into 5cm/2"chunks, season with salt and place in a colander. You'll notice the bitter juices running out of the aubergines as the salt gets to work on them, so put the colander in the sink. I still can't think of any reason why anyone would want to reserve this liquid.

As the vegetables begin to brown, add the tomatoes and stir in. Once cooked down into a thick sauce, add the spices. Stir in over a very gentle heat until the mixture is almost a paste. Add the coriander, apricots and almonds. A quick stir, and now add the pieces of lamb, with the juice that has collected in the bottom of the dish. Stir and make sure the meat is evenly distributed through the mixture. Add the stock just to cover (you may not need all of it). Another quick stir, cover with a lid and place in the oven at 180°C/350°F/gas 4. After 1 hour, rinse the aubergines and squeeze them before adding to the casserole. Leave in the oven for another hour. Remove from the oven, adjust seasoning as necessary, replace lid and allow to relax for 30 minutes before serving.

To serve, place a serving spoon of couscous on a plate and ladle over the casserole, chunky bits and all. Make sure there is plenty of juice to soak up the couscous.

Serves 8

Dessert | Pear and Apple Crumble with Cinnamon and Ice Cream

There is nothing flash about this pudding, but it certainly hits the spot. We hardly ever manage to actually sell any because the staff eat most of it during service. A really good vanilla ice cream far outweighs any clotted cream number or other fancy, expensive complement.

For the Fruit
100g/3^1/$_2$oz butter
100g/3^1/$_2$oz caster sugar
4 green apples, eg Granny Smiths, peeled, cored and cut into 2^1/$_2$cm/1" chunks

6 juicy pears, prepared as the apples above
1 tbsp cinnamon

For the Crumble
250g/9oz unsalted butter

175g/6oz plain flour
175g/6oz Moscavado sugar or brown sugar
100g/3^1/$_2$oz flaked almonds

ice cream, to accompany

Melt 100gms/3^1/$_2$oz butter in a heavy-bottomed pan. Add the sugar and apples and slowly cook. After 5-6 minutes add the pears. After 2 more minutes add the cinnamon and stir in. Tip out into a baking dish.

In a food processor, put the butter, flour, sugar and almonds and pulse until it has the consistency of breadcrumbs. Crumble this mixture over the cooked fruit and place in the oven at 190°C/375°F/gas 5 for approximately 20 minutes or until the top is crispy. Remove the dish from the oven and hide it before serving.

Serves 6

And... | Cracked Wheat Salad

By now most people are familiar with the classic Tuscan bread salad called panzanella. The Italians use stale bread, but here we add a North African twist to it – not only by substituting cracked wheat for the bread but by adding some sweet spices. While it serves as a useful accompaniment to spicy meat dishes, it works just fine on its own. You are aiming for a lush juicy salad.

100ml/4fl oz extra virgin olive oil
50ml/2fl oz balsamic vinegar (use a good one – the great summer vegetables deserve it)
4 cloves of garlic, finely minced
450g/1lb vine tomatoes, the riper the better
2 green peppers
2 red peppers

1 cucumber, peeled & deseeded
handful of basil
handful of mint
handful of coriander

For the cracked wheat
200g/7oz cracked wheat (200g doesn't look a lot, but you'll see)
1 tsp toasted cumin, finely

ground
1 tsp ground coriander
1 tsp ground cinnamon
1 tsp ground ginger
1 tbsp salt (don't be timid)
1 tsp pepper
600ml/1pt boiling water

Whisk the olive oil, garlic and vinegar in a separate bowl.

Coarsely chop all the other non-salad ingredients into a salad bowl with all their juices. Add the dressing, mix it all up by hand and allow to stand for 30 minutes to an hour.

Toss the dry cracked wheat in a bowl with the cumin, coriander, cinnamon, ginger, salt and pepper. Pour over the boiling water and allow to sit somewhere warm, covered with Clingfilm, for 15-20 minutes. Remove the Clingfilm, drain off any excess liquid, and loosen with a fork. Spoon the cracked wheat into the vegetables and allow to stand for another 30 minutes to an hour. The longer you can leave this to stand the better for it!

Serves 8

And...   Smoked Salmon and Rocket Bruschetta with Grilled Red Onion Relish

An easy, quick, yet sexy, snack: folds of sliced smoked salmon on hearty grilled bread with a glossy, green and red speckled salad. Yep, this one made it into our menu book after a great debut on the blackboard.

2 large red onions, peeled
1 large red chilli, seeds removed, and diced
2 tbsp finely chopped parsley
1 tbsp caster sugar
75ml/3fl oz extra virgin olive oil,

and a bit for the bread
50ml/2fl oz balsamic vinegar
several sprigs of flat leaf parsley
salt, preferably Maldon
coarsely ground black pepper
8 slices hearty rustic bread

bread, sliced
garlic head, for bread
smoked salmon, as much as you like

Slice the onions north to south into thin wedges, being sure that the leaves are still held together by the root, so that when you're grilling them it's easy to turn them over. Set the grill at medium heat, not too hot, so that the inside of the wedge can cook and soften. DO NOT BRUSH WITH OLIVE OIL. If you use oil you will only burn your vegetables and start a fire! When you've finished grilling, cover the onions with tin foil for a few minutes.

Meanwhile, mix the chilli, finely chopped parsley, sugar, balsamic and olive oil together. Toss the onions with this mixture – don't they look great? Just before serving toss the sprigs of parsley through the onions.

Grill your bread, smear with a head of garlic and drizzle with oil. Fold some slices of smoked salmon across the bread and now place a sensible handful of the onion relish on top and you're off.

Serves 8

THE FOX INN
Lower Oddington, Gloucestershire

The Fox Inn is one of those picture perfect country pubs that dreams are made of. Just a couple of minutes out of Stow-on-the-Wold, in the exquisite and unspoilt village of Lower Oddington, Sally and Kirk Ritchie's much acclaimed 16th-century inn is the perfect setting for a quintessential British pub of immense charm. Fantastic food from Head Chef Ray Pearce and a remarkable collection of fine wines seems to fit the bill for most. A pretty walled garden with a terrace for fine-weather dining just completes the picture.

Starter	Griddled Scallops with Mizuna, Ginger and Shallot Dressing

For the Dressing
1 knob of root ginger, finely diced
3 shallots, finely diced
4 tbsp peanut oil
4 tbsp walnut oil
1 tbsp soy sauce

1 tbsp lemon juice
4 spring onions, finely diced
sea salt and pepper

For the Scallops
600g/1lb 4oz scallops (allow about 5 or 6 large scallops per person)
peanut oil, for cooking
200g/7oz mizuna or rocket leaves

To make the dressing, cook the ginger and shallot in some of the peanut oil over a low heat until soft. Transfer to a mixing bowl and add the walnut oil, soy sauce, lemon juice, spring onions and the rest of the peanut oil. Whisk together and check the seasoning.

Heat a large frying pan or griddle with a little peanut oil until very hot. Season the scallops and sear in a smoking pan for 1 minute on each side until golden brown.

Arrange the mizuna leaves on the plates. Put the scallops around the side. Spoon the dressing over and serve.

Serves 4

| **Main** | **Braised Lamb Shanks with Lemon Zest and Garlic** |

1 carrot, diced
1 onion, diced
2 celery sticks, diced
olive oil, for cooking
2 tsp chopped thyme
10 garlic cloves, diced

grated zest of 2 lemons
1 tbsp tomato purée
1 x 400g/4oz can of chopped
 tomatoes
1/2 bottle of white wine
300ml/1/2pt veal stock

6 lamb shanks
salt and pepper
2 tsp balsamic vinegar
chopped parsley, to garnish
mashed potatoes and winter
 vegetables, to serve

Cook the vegetables in olive oil over a low heat until tender. Add the thyme, garlic, lemon zest and tomato purée and cook for 2 minutes. Pour in the tomatoes, wine and veal stock. Bring to the boil and simmer.

Season the lamb shanks and brown on all sides in olive oil. Place in the simmering braising liquid. Cover and cook in a preheated oven at 180°C/350°F/gas 4 for about 1 1/2-2 hours until the meat is tender and coming off the bone.

Take the meat out of the pan and boil the liquid until slightly reduced, skimming off any fat from the top with a ladle. Check the seasoning and consistency and add the balsamic vinegar to bring out all the flavours. Serve with mashed potatoes or potato and parsnip mash, plus winter vegetables, adding plenty of chopped parsley before serving.

Serves 6

| **Dessert** | **Banana and Pistachio Filo Parcels with Toffee Sauce** |

115g/4oz butter, melted
4 bananas, sliced
75g/3oz light brown sugar
zest and juice of 1 lemon
75g/3oz pistachio nuts, coarsely

chopped
1 packet of filo pastry, cut into
 12.5cm/5" squares

For the Sauce
225g/8oz butter
350g/12oz dark brown sugar
200ml/7fl oz double cream

Pour half the butter into a frying pan and add the bananas, sugar and lemon zest and juice and cook for 3 minutes. Add the pistachios and remove from the heat.

Brush 3 filo squares with melted butter and layer them to make a star shape. Place 2 tablespoons of the banana mixture in the middle and scrunch the sides together. Brush with butter and place on a baking sheet. Repeat with the remaining filling, pastry and butter to make 6 parcels. Cook the parcels in a preheated oven at 200°/400°F/gas 6 for 15 minutes or until golden brown.

Meanwhile, make the sauce: melt the butter then stir in the sugar until dissolved. Add the cream and cook for 3 minutes. Serve with the parcels.

Serves 6

And... Wilted Rocket, Red Onion, Black Olive and Parmesan Tart

For the Pastry
115g/4oz unsalted butter, diced
250g/9oz plain flour
pinch of salt
1 egg yolk
2 tbsp water

For the Filling
4 red onions, thinly sliced
50g/2oz butter
150g/5oz rocket
6 eggs
250ml/9fl oz double cream

250g/9oz Parmesan cheese, grated
15 pitted black olives
salt and pepper

To make the pastry, rub the butter into the flour and salt until it resembles fine breadcrumbs (or use a food processor or mixer). Add the egg yolk and 2 tablespoons of water and mix quickly until the pastry forms a ball. Cover and refrigerate for at least 1 hour.

Roll out the pastry and use to line a 25cm/10" flan tin. Leave to rest in the refrigerator for another 30 minutes before baking blind in a preheated oven at 180°C/350°F/gas 4 for 20 minutes.

Meanwhile, make the filling: cook the onion in the butter over a low heat until quite soft. Stir in the rocket until wilted. Strain through a colander and squeeze dry.

Beat the eggs with the cream, Parmesan and salt and pepper.

Put the rocket in the pastry case and scatter over the olives. Pour the cream mixture over. Bake in a preheated oven at 200-220°C/400–425°F/gas 6–7 for 30 minutes, turning the temperature down to160-170°C/300-325°F/gas 2-3 as the tart starts to brown. Leave to cool. Serve sliced, either hot or cold.

Serves 8

And... Beetroot Relish

Perfect with duck confit or bangers.

2 large onions, thinly sliced
175g/6oz brown sugar
350ml/12fl oz balsamic vinegar
grated zest and juice of 3

oranges
2 knobs of root ginger, cut into thin strips
175g/6oz currants

2 bay leaves
salt and pepper
6-8 raw beetroots, peeled and cut into thin strips

Mix all the ingredients together except the beetroot. Bring to the boil and simmer for 5 minutes. Add the beetroot and bring back to the boil. Cook, stirring frequently for 30-45 minutes until the beetroot is tender. When the beetroot is almost cooked, strain and then reduce the remaining liquid right down. Add the ingredients back in and check the seasoning.

Either immediately put into scrupulously clean jars, cover with vinegar-proof lids and keep in a cool place for up to 4 months; or leave to cool and keep in a covered bowl in the fridge for up to 2 weeks.

Serves 6

...Specials...

...ased ham hock, leek &
...itake mushroom rissotto £5.25

...led Swordfish with a salad of
...dried tomato, cucumber &
...ves with red onion £11.00

...ked gilthead bream with parsle...
...er & lemon butter
£12.25

WINES

🍷   🍾

...uriz Estate 2000
...donnay, Chile   £3.10   £16.50

...eret Stellenbosch
...th Africa   £2.35   £12.75

THE GRIFFIN INN
Fletching, East Sussex

The Griffin Inn has been a beacon of hospitality in East Sussex for 450 years. It stands proudly in the village of Fletching opposite the 12th-century church where Simon de Montfort prayed before the battle of Lewes in 1264. The food here is rather more up to date however. Jason Williams, the Head Chef, sources the very best local and organic produce. By pub standards this is a big kitchen, with six chefs, constantly producing food of a standard that highlights the revolution that has taken place in British pub cooking over recent years.

Starter	Spicy Crab Beignets with Sweet Chilli Sauce

50g/2oz butter, diced
115g/4oz plain flour
2 eggs, beaten
pinch of salt
450g/1lb cooked crab

1 bunch of spring onions, chopped
15g/$\frac{1}{2}$oz root ginger, grated
1 tsp chopped dill
few drops of Tabasco sauce

1 green pepper, diced
Thai or Chinese chilli dipping sauce, to serve

Bring 150ml/5fl oz water to the boil, add the butter, remove from the heat and stir in the flour. Return the pan to a low heat and cook, stirring vigorously, until the paste comes away from the sides of the pan. Leave to cool slightly before gradually beating in the eggs with the salt to make smooth, stiff and glossy choux pastry.

Mix the remaining ingredients together then add the choux pastry.

Heat a deep pan half-filled with oil to about 180°C/350°F. Add teaspoonfuls of the mixture to the hot oil and fry until brown and crisp; do not overcrowd the pan. Keep warm while frying the remaining mixture. Serve hot with the chilli dipping sauce.

Serves 6

Main	Rosemary and Mustard Crusted Best End of Lamb with Braised Borlotti Beans

1kg/2lb borlotti beans, podded (you could use dried haricot beans, which you would soak in water before use)
6 ripe tomatoes, left whole

1 bunch of sage
4 garlic cloves, left in their skins
sea salt and pepper
chicken stock, to cover
300ml/$\frac{1}{2}$pt extra virgin olive oil

2 tbsp Dijon mustard
3 racks of lamb (French-trimmed)
leaves from 1 bunch of rosemary, finely chopped

Put the beans into a large ovenproof dish about 10cm/4" deep. Add the tomatoes, sage, garlic, cracked black pepper and sea salt. Pour on the chicken stock until it just covers the beans.

Add the olive oil, cover with foil and cook for 1¹/₂ hours, covered, on a low heat or until most of the liquid is absorbed.

Spread the mustard evenly over the lamb and sprinkle over the rosemary. Roast in a preheated oven for 20 minutes. Remove from the oven and leave the lamb to rest for 10 minutes before cutting into individual cutlets. Serve with the beans.

Serves 6

Dessert | Panacotta with Summer Berries

3 leaves of gelatine
2 vanilla pods

850ml/1¹/₂pt double cream
175g/6oz caster sugar, extra for

the berries
250g/8oz mixed summer berries

Soak the gelatine according to the packet instructions. Scrape the seeds from the vanilla pods into the cream then bring to the boil. Add the sugar and gelatine, stir until dissolved then pour into small moulds that have been lined with Clingfilm. Place in the fridge for 2-3 hours.

Put the summer berries into a saucepan with a little sugar and heat through for 2-3 minutes. Ease the panacottas from the moulds on to serving plates and spoon over the summer berries.

Serves 6

And... | Frittata Verdi

asparagus, 2-3 spears per
  person
broad beans, 50g/2oz per
person

fresh peas, 50g/2oz
3 eggs per person
a little grated Parmesan
olive oil

milk, 125ml/4floz per person
basil
rocket leaves and freshly shaved
  Parmesan, to serve

Blanch the vegetables and drain well.

Whisk the eggs with the Parmesan and seasoning. Heat the olive oil in a heavy-bottomed frying pan. Pour in the egg mixture and use a fork to ease the mixture into the middle of the pan until it firms up. Sprinkle the vegetables on top then scatter over the basil. Put in a preheated oven at 110°C/200°F/gas¹/₄ for 10 minutes then finish under a hot grill to brown. Transfer to a plate and serve with rocket leaves and freshly shaved Parmesan.

THE HAVELOCK TAVERN
Masbro Road, London W14

When Jonny Haughton and Peter Richnall opened the Havelock in 1996 their main aim was to serve straightforward, decent cooking to the local community and to do it without too much fuss. And they have succeeded beyond their hopes and they would be the first to concede that much of this is down to their fine team of chefs, notably Jim Garvan, Joanne Wilkinson and Mark Robinson. Menus are changed twice daily at the Havelock and consequently a huge repertoire of dishes has been built up. From a tiny kitchen big miracles are performed - some of these can be realised by the domestic cook through the dishes that have been written for this book.

Starter	Grilled Mackerel with Marinated Fennel and Lemon Salad

This is a beautiful dish with clean, fresh flavours. It works with most oily fish such as sardines and tuna and is simplicity itself to prepare. However, as with all recipes that rely on lemon and garlic, you'll have to exercise a degree of discretion when preparing the salad because, of course, the size of these two ingredients can vary enormously.

2 fennel bulbs
sea salt and pepper
1 garlic clove, finely chopped

juice of $1/2$ lemon
4 mackerel fillets
2 tbsp flat leaf parsley, finely

chopped
6 tbsp extra virgin olive oil

Discard the outer leaves of the fennel if tough or discoloured and then slice thinly. Place in a bowl with a decent pinch of sea salt, the garlic and the lemon juice and toss together. Leave to marinate for 30 minutes.

Meanwhile, prepare the mackerel by removing any bones (tweezers are good for this) and preheat a ridged grill pan or, alternatively, a heavy-bottomed frying pan. Either way, you need to avoid overcrowding the pan when you cook the fish.

Finish the salad by adding the parsley, pepper and olive oil and place on 4 plates. The salad needs to be fairly astringent with a bit of crunch although the lemon juice will have softened the fennel a bit.

Lightly brush the fillets with oil and season on both sides. Cook the fillets skin side down initially for about 1 minute. When the fish looks two-thirds cooked, flip it over for another 30 seconds or so. Prepare yourself for vast amounts of smoke and assure your guests you know what you are doing. Serve with the salad.

Serves 4

| **Main** | **Pot-roast Chicken with Leeks, Anchovy and Garlic** |

This is a Bruno Loubet recipe that I have been cooking for years and which remains an all-time favourite. It is absolutely delicious and for the large numbers of people seemingly averse to anchovies, don't worry, you won't know they are there – just try it. It is essential you find the very best chicken you can for this dish.

4 large, free-range chicken legs
1.25kg/2$\frac{1}{2}$lb leeks, chopped
  into 2.5cm/1" pieces
10 garlic cloves, crushed
1 sprig of rosemary

2 tbsp soy sauce
175ml/6fl oz white wine
50g/2oz anchovies, chopped
2 tbsp parsley, chopped
juice of $\frac{1}{2}$ lemon

salt and pepper
new potatoes and green salad,
  to serve

Colour the chicken legs in olive oil in a heavy ovenproof pot.

Blanch the leeks in plenty of salted water for 3 minutes, drain and add to the chicken. Add the garlic to the pot with the rosemary, soy and wine. Bring to a simmer and don't worry about the lack of liquid – the juices from the leeks and chicken will exude in the cooking process. Seal with a tight-fitting lid and cook in a preheated oven at 200°C/400°F/gas 6 for about 20-25 minutes. Add the anchovies and parsley, stir and return to the oven for another 5 minutes. Check the chicken is done, add the lemon juice and check for salt and pepper. Give a final stir and serve with new potatoes and a green salad.

Serves 4

| **Dessert** | **Blood Orange Salad with Ricard and Mint** |

I have never fully understood why there are so many people in this country who dislike aniseed when just over the channel you find the exact opposite. Is it the weather possibly or something in the air? If, like me, you hate the stuff as well, please do nonetheless try it as this is a great dish, simple yet delicious. It always evokes happy memories of my first cooking job at Le Bouchon Lyonnais where, as the only non-Frenchman, I was occasionally allowed to go near the food. The common version is to set the juices into a light jelly which you can easily do by warming them up with some gelatine. I don't particularly like jelly so I serve it as it is.

2 tbsp sugar
1 tsp Ricard

10 blood oranges
10 mint leaves, finely shredded

Dissolve the sugar in 4 tbsp water over a low heat. Remove from the heat, add the Ricard and leave to cool.

Meanwhile, cut off the orange peel with a sharp knife, leaving no trace of pith. Slice the oranges horizontally into 4 or 5 slices, remove the pips and pour over the Ricard syrup. Cover and leave to macerate in the fridge for 30 minutes. Serve chilled with finely shredded mint scattered over.

Serves 4

And...	# Spiced Red Lentils with Coriander and Yoghurt

I hesitate to call this a dhal because I am not an Indian and thus cannot claim to fully understand the subtle complexities of their spicing but this is a dish which can produce raptures in certain people and that is good enough for me. We sometimes serve this dish as a little starter with perhaps some homemade roti or as part of an Indian vegetarian main course with some pilau rice and possibly a bhaji of some sort. It also makes an excellent garnish for grilled or fried fish like cod, monkfish or scallops when we would add some lightly cooked spinach. A word of warning: it is easy to make this dish slightly too intense so a little goes a long way! There are various stages to this recipe, none particularly difficult, but this is a dish that requires plenty of attention. There are two things vital for success: firstly use a heavy-bottomed pot and secondly you must stir it every 5 minutes or so to avoid it catching.

150g/5oz red lentils
1 carrot, coarsely grated
1 onion, finely chopped
4 tbsp vegetable oil
2.5cm/1" piece root ginger, chopped
6 garlic cloves, chopped
1 tsp ground turmeric
200g/7oz canned

tomatoes, chopped
1 small bunch of coriander
juice of $1/2$ lemon
salt and pepper
100ml/$3^1/2$fl oz coconut milk (optional)

For the Spice Mixture
1 tbsp cumin seeds

1 tbsp coriander seeds
1 tbsp yellow mustard seeds
1 tsp cardamom seeds
1 bay leaf
1 dried red chilli
4 cloves
2.5cm/1" cinnamon stick
2 tsp black peppercorns

Soak the lentils in cold water for at least 30 minutes.

Meanwhile, put the spice mixture ingredients into a heavy pan and 'dry-fry' (i.e. no oil) until the seeds begin to pop and you start to get a fragrant spice aroma. Do this over a gentle heat as even slightly over-roasted spices will overpower the dish. Now grind the mix in a pestle and mortar or, probably easier, in an electric grinder. Stand back and marvel at the smell.

Start frying the onion and carrot in the oil in a heavy-bottomed pan over a moderate heat, stirring from time to time until you have a darkly golden, slightly sticky mass. While this is happening, purée the ginger and garlic with 500ml/18fl oz water in a blender until smooth. (Alternatively, you can finely grate the ginger and garlic separately.)

When the onion mix is almost done, add the turmeric and cook for a minute or two over a low heat. The difficult bit is now over as you simply add the drained lentils, tomatoes, garlic, ginger, spices and water and bring to a boil.

Tie up the coriander stalks (make sure they are well washed), add to the pot and simmer over the lowest possible heat until the lentils are completely broken down, a process than can take from anything up to 2 hours.

Season with lemon juice and salt and, if you prefer a less gutsy version, add the coconut milk to round things off. Garnish with a scattering of coriander leaves and some natural yoghurt. This is a dish best served warm.

Serves 4

And...   Elderflower Cordial

Nothing quite ushers in the summer better than a glass of home-made elderflower soda and towards the end of May, you will find me down at the local pharmacy trying to persuade the manager to hand over industrial quantities of tartaric acid for this heady brew. As he suspects we are in the exciting business of producing crack cocaine, normally it is a bit of a struggle!

1kg/2lb granulated sugar
15 large elderflower heads, stalks removed, heads well shaken

2 oranges, thinly sliced
2 lemons, thinly sliced

2 limes, thinly sliced
25g/1oz tartaric acid

Bring the sugar and 1l/1³⁄₄pt water to the boil. Add the elderflowers and return to the boil. Pour over the rest of the ingredients and leave to steep for 24 hours. Strain through muslin and store in a cool place – it will keep indefinitely. It's that simple!

THE HOSTE ARMS
Burnham Market, Norfolk

Situated on The Green in the delightful village of Burnham Market, The Hoste Arms has probably one of the most envied reputations for the quality of its food in the country and is a fine example of how good food, accommodation and pubby facilities can be offered in one place. Like so many of the best real food pubs, the kitchen uses the freshest, seasonal local produce – the Burnham Creek oysters are fantastic.

Starter | Fricassee of Seafood

4 lime leaves, chopped
1 lemon grass stalk, crushed
2 garlic cloves, cut in half and chopped
50g/2oz root ginger, chopped
100ml/3$\frac{1}{2}$fl oz white wine
200ml/7fl oz fish stock

2 tins of coconut milk
75g/3oz tomato purée
50g/2oz tom yam paste
200ml/7fl oz double cream
600g/1lb 5oz cod, salmon, bass, fresh tuna, mussels, your choice, skin on, cut into

2cm/$\frac{3}{4}$" dice
2 heads of pak choi, finely chopped
50g/2oz mangetout, finely chopped
50g/2oz beansprouts
chopped coriander, to garnish

Put the lime leaves, lemon grass, garlic and ginger in a saucepan with the white wine and reduce by half. Add fish stock and reduce by half again. Then add the coconut milk, tomato paste and tom yam paste, bring to the boil and simmer for 10 minutes. Pass through a strainer and return to the pan. Add the cream and reheat gently. Season to taste.

Meanwhile, bring a pan of seasoned water or fish stock to boil. Poach the fish for a few minutes. When just about ready, add the vegetables and cook for 30 seconds. Drain and add to the bisque. Serve garnished with chopped coriander.

Serves 6

Main | Roast Fillet of Beef with Mushroom and Herb Pancake Galette

For the Pancake Galette
150ml/5fl oz milk
100g/3$\frac{1}{2}$oz plain flour
3 eggs
450g/1lb fresh herbs, finely chopped
salt and pepper

For the Mushrooms
150g/5oz butter
1 onion, finely chopped
1kg/2lb mushrooms, roughly chopped
4 sprigs of tarragon
salt and pepper

1 whole fillet of beef
batons of carrot, mooli, parsnip and beetroot, blanched then fried in butter and oil, to serve

To make the herb pancakes, whisk the milk, flour, eggs, herbs and seasoning together until smooth. Heat some vegetable oil in a frying pan and add some of the mixture. Cook until the pancake is set. Repeat, you need to make about 7 pancakes.

To make the mushroom filling, fry all the ingredients together until the mushrooms are very soft. Drain off the excess juices, discard the tarragon, season and blend the vegetables to a pulp in a food processor.

To assemble the galette, place a pancake on a board, spread on mushroom filling, cover with another pancake and continue until all the pancakes and filling have been used. Refrigerate and then with a sharp knife cut into wedges like a cake.

Roast the beef in a preheated oven 220°C/425°F/gas 7 to your liking. Just before the beef is done, fry the blanched vegetables in butter and oil and set aside. Gently heat the galette wedges and serve with the vegetables and any gravy you have made from the juices in the roasting pan.

Serves 10

Dessert | Chocolate Lasagne with Chocolate Mousse and Cherries

325g/13oz plain chocolate, chopped
65g/2$\frac{1}{2}$oz caster sugar
6 egg yolks
650ml/1$\frac{1}{4}$pt double cream, half-whipped
icing sugar, for dusting
mint, to decorate

For the Chocolate Sauce
450g/1lb sugar
460ml/16fl oz water
175g/6oz cocoa powder
115g/4oz plain chocolate, chopped

For the Chocolate Pasta
325g/11oz plain strong white flour

25g/1oz cocoa powder
3 eggs, beaten

stock syrup, made from 1l/2pt water and 200g/7oz sugar
2 split vanilla pods
2 oranges, quartered
1 stick cinnamon
450g/1lb griotines cherries (ready macerated in wine)

Melt the chocolate in a basin placed over, not in, a saucepan of hot water. Dissolve the sugar in 65ml/2$\frac{1}{2}$fl oz water over a low heat, stirring. Bring to the boil without stirring and boil for 1 minute. Leave to cool slightly then whisk with the yolks until pale, light and aerated in a large bowl over another pan of hot water. Fold in the chocolate and cream. Transfer to a bowl or tub and leave to set.

Make the chocolate sauce: put the ingredients into a pan and bring to the boil. Leave to cool.

To make the chocolate pasta, sift the flour and cocoa into the bowl of a food mixer or processor. Add the eggs and mix with the dough hook or blade until the mixture comes to a well worked dough. Wrap in Clingfilm, and leave to rest. Roll out the dough very thin (2mm or number 1 setting on the pasta machine) and cut into 5cm/2" rounds, allowing 3 per person.

Bring the syrup to the boil, without stirring and boil for a minute. Add the vanilla, orange and cinnamon. Lower the heat so the syrup just simmers, add the pasta and poach for 1 minute or until it swells. Lift out with a fish slice and drain on a cloth. Leave to cool in the fridge. To serve, spoon the chocolate mousse in a piping bag and pipe a small ball of mousse on a disc of pasta then put a layer of pasta on top. Add another ball of mousse and sprinkle with cherries. Finish with a layer of pasta. Pour the chocolate sauce over and around. Dust with icing sugar and decorate with mint.

Serves 12

And...   Hoste Arms Beef Burgers

20g/³/₄oz diced onion
oil, for cooking
250g/9oz minced rump steak
1¹/₂ tbsp Dijon mustard
1¹/₂ tbsp tomato ketchup

1 tsp mixed herbs, finely
  chopped
splash of Worcestershire sauce
salt and pepper

To Serve
toasted sesame bun
grated Monterey Jack cheese
pancetta, fried until crisp

Fry the onion in a little oil until softened and lightly coloured. Drain on paper towels then mix with the remaining ingredients.

Form the mixture into burgers. Fry or grill to your liking. Serve in toasted sesame bun with Monterey Jack cheese and crisp fried pancetta.

Serves 1

And...   Fig and Grape Chutney

4 chillies, deseeded and
  chopped
2 pieces of ginger root, finely
  chopped
2 apples, peeled, cored and

chopped
3.6kg/8lb black seedless grapes
oil, for cooking
450g/1lb sugar
550ml/1pt best quality malt

vinegar
1 x 500g/18oz jar of baby figs,
  marinated in stock syrup
1.2l/2pt stock syrup

Cook the chillies, ginger, apples and grapes in a little oil over a low heat until soft. Add the sugar and vinegar. Boil until reduced down to a glaze, so that nearly all the liquid has gone. Add the stock syrup and the figs and reduce to a chutney consistency. Store in Kilner jars where the chutney will keep for up to three months.

Makes 1.5kg/3 lb

THE HUNDRED HOUSE HOTEL
Norton, Shropshire

It's a family affair at the Hundred House - Henry and Sylvia Phillips and sons David and Stuart have been running food-driven pubs for the last 25 years and creating something of a culinary legend at this landmark Shropshire inn since 1986. Stuart Phillips has worked in Michelin starred kitchens in France as well as doing a stint at Rowley Leigh's legendary Kensington Place restaurant in Notting Hill in the early 1990s. The pub's food is based very much on local produce as well as herbs from Sylvia's immense gardens. Stuart Phillips' menus offer the best of whatever is available: wild boar, Shropshire lamb, Hereford ducks, Brixham fish. Wonderful food served in atmospheric surroundings and a beacon for everything that is good and exciting about British pub food.

Starter   Chicken and Cream Cheese Terrine

3 skinless chicken breasts
juice of 1 small lime
25ml/1fl oz brandy
125g/4oz minced belly of pork
oil, for frying
500g/10oz cream cheese
grated zest and juice of $^1/_2$

lemon
1 garlic clove, finely crushed
25g/1oz sage leaves, thinly
  sliced
25g/1oz spring onions, thinly
  sliced
1 egg, beaten

salt and pepper
streaky bacon
salad, toasted country bread
  and Muscat grapes macerated
  in white port, to serve

Beat out the chicken breasts lightly and lay in a shallow, non-metallic dish. Pour over the lime juice and brandy, cover and marinate overnight in the fridge.

Fry the pork in a little oil over a fairly low heat, stirring to break up the meat, until crisp. Tip into a colander and leave to drain and cool.

Mix together the pork, cream cheese, lemon zest and juice, garlic, sage, spring onions, eggs and seasoning. Line 2 terrines with plenty of thinly rolled streaky bacon. Spread a 1.25cm/$^1/_2$" layer of the cream cheese mixture in the base of each terrine. Add 3 chicken breasts and repeat. Top with enough cheese mixture to bring about 2-2.5cm/$^3/_4$-1" above the terrine lip. Interleaf bacon over the top to seal in the filling. Bake in a bain-marie in a preheated oven at 180°C/350°F/gas 4 for 1 hour 10 minutes. Baking the terrines uncovered browns the top giving a more savoury flavour.

Remove the terrines from the bain-marie and leave to cool. Put a tray or plate on top and weight with about 1$^1/_2$lb. Leave overnight in a cool place. Serve sliced and accompanied by salad, toasted country bread and Muscat grapes macerated in white port.

Serves 10

Main	Roast Pork with Fennel and Black Olives

1$^1/_2$ fennel bulbs, quartered
olive oil for cooking
1 tbsp coriander seeds
$^3/_4$ tsp fennel seeds
$^3/_4$ tsp black pepper
$^3/_4$ tsp sea salt
2 small eggs, beaten
1 red onion, finely chopped
zest of 1 orange

juice of 1$^1/_2$ oranges
1 tbsp chopped parsley
2 garlic cloves, minced
175g/6oz black olives, halved
450g/1lb minced pork
2.4-2.6kg/5-6lb loin of pork with
  skin and about half the belly
  attached
mirepoix of vegetables, (carrot,

celery, onion, chopped into fine
  dice)
pork bones
white wine, to deglaze
light, brown stock
lemon zest
sage leaves, chopped

Brush the fennel with olive oil, put in an oiled baking or roasting tin, then roast in a preheated oven at 220°C/425°F/gas 7 for about 35 minutes or until tender. Leave to cool on a wire rack.

Roast the coriander and fennel seeds in a heavy, dry, frying pan until fragrant, then blitz them with the pepper and salt in a spice grinder. Mix thoroughly with the remaining ingredients, except the joint and fennel, mirepoix, bones, wine, stock, zest and sage.

Score the pork skin and make a pocket near the eye of the loin. Remove the excess fat. Bat out the belly pork to lengthen it. Place one third of the stuffing into the pocket next to the eye of the loin. Press in the cooked fennel and then add the rest of the stuffing. Roll the belly flap over so that the loin is now round with the roast fennel roughly in the centre. Tie along the length of the joint with string and place in a roasting tin with the bones and mirepoix. Roast in a preheated oven at 180°C/350°F/gas 4 for 2$^1/_2$ hours.

Remove the pork from the oven and leave to rest for 15 minutes. Tip everything into a clean pan and deglaze with some white wine. Add some light, brown stock and cook until reduced. Pass through a strainer and add some lemon zest and chopped sage. Check seasoning before serving with the pork.

Serves 12

Dessert | Coconut Cake with Tropical Fruit Salad and Passion-fruit Syrup

For the Cake
165g/5$\frac{1}{2}$oz caster sugar
150g/5oz self-raising flour
45g/1$\frac{3}{4}$oz desiccated coconut
125g/4$\frac{1}{2}$oz butter, melted
1 egg, beaten
50ml/2fl oz milk
50ml/2fl oz coconut milk

For the Passion-fruit Syrup
225ml/8fl oz passion-fruit pulp
165g/5$\frac{1}{2}$oz caster sugar
50ml/2fl oz lime juice
50ml/2fl oz water
1 vanilla pod

For the Fruit Salad
400g/14oz peeled, cored
   and sliced pineapple
2 star fruit, sliced
8 lychees, peeled and
   stones removed
$\frac{1}{2}$ papaya, peeled and
   seeds removed

Combine the sugar, flour and desiccated coconut in a bowl. Stir in the butter, egg, milk and coconut milk and mix well. Spoon into a greased and lined cake tin 20cm/8" and bake in a preheated oven at 180°C/350°F/gas 4 for 30 minutes. Leave the cake to stand in the tin for 10 minutes before turning on to a wire rack to cool.

To make the passion-fruit syrup, mix the passion-fruit pulp in a food processor for 30 seconds using the pulse button. Strain. Combine the sugar, lime juice and 50ml/2fl oz water in a saucepan. Stir over a low heat until the sugar has dissolved. Add the passion-fruit juice and vanilla pod and simmer without stirring for 10 minutes until thickened slightly.

Mix the fruits together and pour over half the syrup. Serve slices of cake topped with the fruit salad and drizzled with some of the remaining syrup.

Serves 12

And... | Cotriade (Breton Potato and Fish Stew)

For the Saffron Mayonnaise
small pinch of saffron strands
   soaked in 2 tbsp fish stock
2 egg yolks
25g/1oz cooked potato
1 garlic clove crushed
juice of 1$\frac{1}{2}$ lemons
300ml/1$\frac{1}{2}$pt fruity olive oil

For the Stew
4 shallots, thinly sliced
1 garlic clove, sliced
1 sprig of thyme
$\frac{1}{2}$ tbsp butter
$\frac{1}{4}$ bottle of white wine
600ml/1pt fish stock
225g/8oz floury potatoes such
   as Maris Piper, cut into
   1.25cm/$\frac{1}{2}$" thick batons

salt and pepper
350g/12oz mixed fish fillets,
   (usually monkfish, gurnard,
   bass and mullet), cut into
   2.5cm/1" pieces
225g/8oz butter clams
4 large langoustines
chopped chives, parsley and
   sorrel, to serve

To make the saffron mayonnaise, soak the saffron strands in 2 tablespoons of fish stock. Then put into a blender with the egg yolk, potato, garlic and lemon juice. With the motor running, slowly pour in the olive oil. Season to taste. Set aside.

Cook the shallots, garlic and thyme in the butter over a low heat until soft. Add the wine and boil until reduced by half then pour in the fish stock. Bring to the boil and add the potatoes and seasoning. Cook gently until tender.

Leave the potatoes to cool in the poaching liquor then remove to a casserole. Add the fish and shellfish, pour over the stock and bring to a simmer. Cover with the lid and cook for 3-4 minutes until the clams open and the fish is cooked through. Lift everything out of the stock and place in warmed bowls. Sprinkle with the chopped chives, sorrel and parsley.

Remove the pan of cotriade cooking liquid from the heat and stir in 1-2 tablespoons saffron mayonnaise. Return to the heat and cook gently, stirring, until lightly thickened. Pour over the fish and serve.

Serves 6

And... Rocket, Potato and Goats' Cheese Pizza

75ml/3fl oz milk
10g/^{1}/4oz yeast
225g/8oz strong flour
1 egg, beaten
2 tbsp olive oil
pinch of salt

For the Topping
2 waxy potatoes
2 red onions, sliced
olive oil, for cooking and to
  drizzle
rocket, preferably quite leggy but
  not tough

goats' cheese log, peeled and
  thinly sliced
salt flakes and black pepper

rocket mixed with chives, and
  sorrel and rosemary vinaigrette,
  to serve

Whisk the milk into the yeast then pour into a mixing bowl and add the flour, eggs, olive oil and salt. Work for 10 minutes until the dough is smooth and elastic. Roll the dough into a ball, put into an oiled plastic bag and leave to prove until doubled in size.

Meanwhile, make the topping: steam the potatoes until tender, leave until cool enough to handle then slice them very thinly. Fry the red onions in a little olive oil until softened but not coloured.

Drain on paper towels.

Knock the dough back and roll it into a log. Divide into 50g/2oz balls and roll each out 3 mm/^{1}/8" thick. Top with plenty of rocket, then potato followed by onion and, lastly, goats' cheese. Sprinkle over salt flakes and black pepper. Drizzle lightly with olive oil and bake on a stone or a solid metal tray in a preheated oven at 200°C/400°F/gas 6 for about 10-12 minutes until blistered and crisp, the rocket sunk and the cheese melted.

Place a ball of the rocket and chive mixture in the centre of each pizza and drizzle with sorrel and rosemary vinaigrette.

Makes 8 pizzas

THE IVY HOUSE
Chalfont St Giles, Buckinghamshire

Buckinghamshire is a famously beautiful county and The Ivy House, close to Chalfont St Giles, must be one of the prettiest pubs within its boundaries. This is a pub for people who love and know about cask-conditioned ales and top-notch wines and who want the food to match them. A serious kitchen, constantly experimenting and perfecting classic dishes with a modern twist – a kitchen striving for something a little bit different, not afraid to plunder the riches of world cooking for the pleasure of their diners.

Starter   Ragout of Wild Mushrooms

The unusual combination of cracked pepper and fresh Parmesan gives a real bite to this creamy dish. It is ideal as a starter, but could also be served as a vegetarian main course for 3 people. Exotic mushrooms come in all shapes and sizes; you can use any type for this recipe or simply stick to small button mushrooms but don't use field or dark mushrooms because the sauce will be grey. Generally, all button mushrooms should be sliced with a knife but the more unusually-shaped mushrooms are best pulled apart gently.

2 onions, diced
oil, for cooking
1 tsp plain flour
500g/1lb 2oz wild or exotic
   mushrooms, chopped or pulled
apart into small pieces,
   according to type
1 vegetable stock cube
1 tsp mixed dried herbs
2 garlic cloves, crushed
1 small glass of white wine
2 tsp cracked pepper
500ml/18fl oz double cream
75g/3oz Parmesan cheese,
   freshly grated

Fry the onions in a little oil in a large saucepan until soft, adding the flour at the last minute to lightly coat. Add the mushrooms, stock cube, herbs, garlic, wine and 500ml/18fl oz water. Simmer until the stock cube has dissolved. Add the pepper and cream and warm through. Leave to cool slightly before adding half the Parmesan. Spoon into shallow bowls and sprinkle with the remaining Parmesan.

Serve and enjoy with fresh crusty bread to mop up the juices.

Serves 6

Main — Beef and Murphy's Casserole with Kumquats

This dish has followed me around and is often used as an example of the food we do at The Ivy House. It is a real winter warmer which mixes traditional with more modern flavours.

500g/1lb 4oz good quality
  braising beef, cut into
  2.5cm/1" cubes
oil, for cooking
3 onions, diced

1.5l/3pt beef or veal stock
2 tsp mixed dried herbs
3 garlic cloves, crushed
250ml/9fl oz Murphy's stout
250ml/9fl oz orange juice

salt and pepper
3 tbsp cornflour
4-5 kumquats, sliced
slices of raw kumquats, to
  garnish

Brown the beef in a little oil in a flameproof casserole or a saucepan, ensuring the beef is sealed on all sides. Add the onion and stir until softened. Stir in the stock and bring to the boil. Lower the heat to a steady simmer and cook for 1-2 hours or until the meat is really tender. It takes time so don't be tempted to rush. Add more water if the beef starts to go dry. Add the herbs, garlic, Murphy's and orange juice. Season and simmer for a few more minutes.

Blend the cornflour with a little cold water then stir into the casserole. Add the kumquats and cook, stirring until thickened. Serve garnished with slices of raw kumquats.

Serves 4-6

Dessert — Mini Pavlova with Toasted Nuts and Sticky Toffee Sauce

This is a must for every sweet tooth in the country – we make it, we sell it, what more needs to be said. Of course, you could cheat and buy ready-made meringue nests, but the real things are hard to beat and if you make extra they last a long time when kept in an airtight container in a dry cupboard.

3 egg whites
175g/6oz caster sugar, sifted
1 tsp cornflour
1/4 tsp vanilla essence
1 tsp lemon juice

For the Toffee Sauce
75g/3oz caster sugar
150ml/5fl oz double cream
50g/2oz unsalted butter, diced

For the Topping
250ml/9fl oz double cream,
  whipped
75g/3oz flaked almonds, toasted
75g/3oz hazelnuts, toasted,
  skinned and halved

Draw 6 circles measuring 7.5-10cm/3-4" in diameter on the wrong side of non-stick baking parchment so that the circles show through on the right side. Oil lightly so the parchment will stick to a baking sheet; put it on the baking sheet.

Whisk the egg whites until very stiff and dry. Whisk in half the sugar and continue whisking until the mixture is stiff and shiny.

Mix the remaining sugar with the cornflour and gently fold into the egg whites with the vanilla essence and lemon juice. Either spoon into a large piping bag fitted with a large nozzle and pipe the nests using the pencil lines as a guide or spoon the meringue to fill the circles, bringing up the sides to create a neat shape. Bake in a cool oven for $1^{1}/_{4}$–$1^{1}/_{2}$ hours until firm and delicately cream in colour. Allow to cool then remove from the baking parchment and store in an airtight container until required.

To make the sauce, dissolve the sugar in 3 tbsp water over a low heat, then bring quickly to the boil and boil until the syrup becomes a deep caramel. Quickly whisk in the cream and butter; the sauce will become lumpy at first but it will soon become smooth and shiny. Leave to cool and store in an airtight jug, or with the surface of the sauce covered closely.

To serve the meringues, put a small dollop of cream on the underside of each meringue nest and place in the centre of each serving plate; this stops the nest sliding around. Pipe the cream into the nests, bringing it up to a peak to make a round cone (or round pyramid-type shape). Warm the toffee sauce if it has become too firm to pour (a few seconds in a microwave will do). Pour toffee sauce over the top of each meringue, allowing it to drizzle down several sides of the 'pyramid'. Sprinkle with the toasted nuts.

Serves 6

And...   Chunky Tomato and Coriander Sauce

A truly simple sauce bursting with flavour, and wonderful with chicken or fish – our favourite is with char-grilled swordfish steak.

500g/18oz jar of quality tomato passata	$^{1}/_{2}$ vegetable stock cube	2 tsp cornflour
2 tomatoes, diced (seeds and skin add flavour and texture)	50ml/2fl oz red wine	1 small bunch of coriander, coarsely chopped
	salt and pepper	
	1 tsp caster sugar	

Put the passata, tomatoes, vegetable stock cube, red wine, seasoning and sugar in a pan and bring to the boil then allow to simmer for a few minutes to let the vegetable stock dissolve and the flavours develop.

Cream the cornflour with 50ml/2fl oz water then stir into the sauce. Simmer, stirring, until thickened. Just before serving, stir in the coriander. Serve hot as required.

Serves 6-8

| **And...** | **Chilli and Sweet Pepper Salsa** |

A feast of colour and flavour that just leaps out of the bowl. This quantity makes a lot, which is ideal for a party. Alternatively, the amount can be halved and kept sealed in the fridge to use over several days.

1 red pepper, finely diced
1 green pepper, finely diced
2 tomatoes, finely diced
1 red onion, finely diced

$1/4$ cucumber, finely diced
250g/9oz tomato passata
2 tsp chopped herbs
$1/2$ tsp Tabasco sauce

2 garlic cloves, crushed
3 tbsp lemon juice
3 tbsp lime juice

Mix all the ingredients together. Serve as a dip with crudités, or warmed with Cajun-spiced fish, or with a mixture of Mexican dishes.

THE JOLLY SPORTSMAN
East Chiltington, East Sussex

Bruce Wass acquired this charming village pub whilst still cooking at his landmark restaurant, Thackerays, in Tunbridge Wells. He sold the restaurant in mid-2001 and is now concentrating exclusively on The Jolly Sportsman. Sympathetically restored to a stylish Victorian dining-room with a pretty cottagey garden in the front, the Jolly Sportsman is causing a stir in local and national food circles. Bruce Wass is one of the country's top chefs and his decision to throw his talents into the kitchens of his pub perfectly illustrates the way that things are changing in the world of both restaurants and real pub food.

Starter | Wood Pigeon and Cep Risotto

For the Risotto
2 shallots, chopped
115g/4oz arborio rice
1 glass of white wine
300ml/$\frac{1}{2}$pt chicken stock
50g/2oz butter, diced, plus extra

for frying
50g/2oz Parmesan, grated

4 plump wood pigeon breasts
oil. for cooking
salt and pepper

4 ceps, sliced
small glass of Madeira
2 tbsp strong game stock
extra virgin olive oil, for drizzling

To make the risotto, fry the shallots in a little butter until soft, then stir in the rice. Add the wine and boil until evaporated. Add one third of the stock, simmer until that has evaporated. Repeat with another two batches of stock. By the end the rice should be moist, creamy and just tender.

A short while before the risotto is ready, fry the pigeon breasts in a little oil until they are cooked pink. Season and leave to rest.

Fry the ceps in oil.

Put the Madeira in a small pan and boil until reduced by half, and then add the game stock.

Slice the pigeon breasts.

Finish the risotto by stirring in the Parmesan and butter. Divide among 4 warm plates and scatter over the pigeon breasts and ceps. Drizzle with the game sauce and then a little olive oil.

Serves 4 as a starter

Main — Chermoula Grilled Tuna

For the Chermoula
small handful of coriander
small handful of parsley
2 garlic cloves, crushed
1 small onion, chopped
$1/2$ tbsp turmeric

$1/2$ tbsp ground cumin
$1/8$ tbsp chilli powder
$1/4$ tbsp paprika
$1/4$ tbsp sea salt
juice of $1/2$ lemon
75ml/3fl oz olive oil

For the rest of the dish
4 x 175g/6oz tuna steaks
olive oil, for cooking
salad and lemon wedges,
 to serve

Grind all the herbs, spices and seasoning in a food processor and then add the lemon juice and olive oil to emulsify.

Lay the tuna in a shallow dish, add the chermoula so the tuna is completely covered and leave to marinate in the fridge overnight.

Heat a little olive oil in a heavy-based frying pan, add the tuna and fry over a high heat for 45 seconds. Turn the tuna over and cook for a further 45 seconds. Serve with salad and lemon wedges.

Serves 4

Dessert — Apricot, Walnut, Ginger and Toffee Pudding

225g/8oz caster sugar
175g/6oz butter
4 eggs, beaten
225g/8oz dried apricots, halved

550g/1lb 3oz self-raising flour (half white, half brown)
2 tsp bicarbonate of soda
550ml/1pt boiling water

2 tsp vanilla essence
2 tbsp ground ginger
175g/6oz walnuts

Cream together the caster sugar and butter until fluffy. Add the beaten eggs slowly.

In a separate bowl coat the apricots in 115g/4oz of the flour, add the bicarbonate of soda and the boiling water.

Add the rest of the flour, the vanilla and ginger to the butter, sugar and egg mixture and at the same time add the apricot batter mix. Fold in the walnuts. Turn into 30 x 20 x 5cm/12 x 8 x 2" tin. Bake at 190°C/375°F/gas 5 for 1-1$1/2$ hours. Test it with a knife as you would a fruit cake, so that the knife comes out clean when cooked. This pudding freezes well.

Serves 20

And... Dickey's Spicy Chutney

This makes a large quality of chutney. For the pub this would stretch to about 100 ploughmans! Just halve or quarter the ingredients if you or your loved one are not members of ploughman's anonymous.

1kg/2lb onions, chopped
oil, for cooking
$1^1/_2$ tbsp cayenne
$2^1/_2$ tbsp salt
1 tbsp English mustard
$^1/_2$ tsp ground ginger
$^1/_2$ tsp fenugreek seeds

$1^1/_2$ tsp coriander seeds
$1^1/_2$ tsp nutmeg
$^1/_2$ tsp ground cardamom
3 large red chillies, chopped
1.5l/$2^3/_4$pt white wine vinegar
450g/1lb plum tomatoes,
  chopped

225g/8oz sultanas
1.1kg/$2^1/_2$lb sharp apples,
chopped
450g/1lb muscovado sugar
50g/2oz capers

Cook the onions in a little oil over a low heat in a large, non-aluminium pan for 20 minutes. Add the spices and vinegar and boil until reduced by two thirds. Add all the remaining ingredients and cook, stirring if necessary to prevent sticking, until there is no free liquid.

Ladle into very clean jars and seal the tops. Label and store in a cool, dark, dry place for up to three months.

Makes 6 large kilner jars

NANTYFFIN CIDER MILL
Crickhowell, Powys

Originally a 16th-century drovers' inn, The Nantyffin, set in the stunning Usk Valley, has long been associated with fine pub food. The inn was producing its own cider right up to the 1960s and the restored cider press and wheel are now a central feature of the dining room. Sean Gerrard and Glyn and Jess Bridgeman took over the inn in 1990 and since that time have firmly established it as one of the finest places to eat in Wales. The three share a passion for real pub food, placing the emphasis on locally produced ingredients enhanced with contemporary flavours from around the world.

Dessert	Stuffed Mushrooms with Stilton Rarebit Topping

The rarebit recipe makes more than you need but grilled on wholemeal bread with a couple of bacon rashers makes for a tasty supper.

For the Filling
450g/1lb minced pork
olive oil, for cooking
1 white onion or 8 shallots, chopped
leaves from a bunch of thyme
4 garlic cloves, chopped
3 Granny Smith apples, peeled, cored and grated
300ml/$\frac{1}{2}$pt dry to medium cider
salt and pepper
175g/6oz Cheddar cheese

For the Rarebit
150g/5oz Cheddar cheese, grated
150g/5oz Stilton, grated
65ml/$2\frac{1}{2}$fl oz milk
25g/1oz fresh white breadcrumbs
25g/1oz flour
dash of Worcestershire sauce
$\frac{1}{2}$ tsp Dijon mustard
2 egg yolks, lightly beaten
1 whole egg, lightly beaten

For the rest of the dish
4 Portabello mushrooms or flat mushrooms
oil or melted butter, for brushing
chopped chives and dressed salad leaves, to serve

Fry the pork in small batches in a little olive oil (this helps to break it up easily). Return all the meat to the pan, cover, reduce the heat and cook for about 20 minutes. Tip the meat and juices into a colander to drain off excess fat and liquid.

In a separate pan, sauté the shallots, half the thyme, the garlic and apple until soft but not coloured. Pour in the cider and boil until reduced completely. Stir in the pork and cook for about 15 minutes. Check the seasoning, add the rest of the thyme and the cheese.

To make the rarebit, gently heat the Cheddar and Stilton in the milk until melted, stir continuously and take care that it does not boil. Stir in the flour, breadcrumbs, mustard and Worcestershire sauce until the mixture leaves the sides of the pan. Pour into a food processor or mixing bowl and leave to cool. Add the egg yolks and eggs in a steady stream. The mixture will be soft but not sticky, and easily pliable.

To serve, brush the mushrooms with oil or melted butter, and grill for 1-2 minutes on each side. Place a small amount of the pork into the cup of the mushroom creating a slightly raised dome effect. With a spatula, spread the rarebit mix over the mince to completely cover it and form a seal around the mushrooms. Cook in a preheated oven at 180-190°C/350-375°F/gas 4-5 for about 15 minutes until the rarebit is glazed and brown; at this point the mince inside will also be hot.

Serve with a sprinkle of chives, and dressed salad leaves.

Serves 4

Main | Confit of Welsh Lamb

Being in a premier location for lamb, during the season we buy the whole carcasses. This recipe was developed to use some of the cheaper cuts of meat. We have taken the French method of confit, which is famous for duck, and used its principles in this lamb dish. The meat is dry marinated for 24 hours and then cooked in duck or goose fat on a very low heat for 4-5 hours to impart a rich succulence, and render out most of the fat. This is a time consuming dish but the benefit is that it can be done in several stages over a number of days and the keeping properties are excellent.

For the Lamb
1.4kg/3lb boneless shoulder of lamb
50g/2oz sea salt
50g/2oz rosemary
1 head of garlic, chopped
pepper
2 x 200g/7oz cans duck or goose fat

For the Mash
450g/1lb peeled floury potatoes (preferably Maris Piper)
225g/8oz butter
25g/1oz chopped rosemary
25g/1oz chopped flat leaf parsley
25g/1oz chopped thyme
25g/1oz chopped chives
salt & pepper

For the Sauce
450g/1lb chopped mixed carrots, onions and celery
1 garlic clove, chopped
1 bunch of rosemary, chopped
1 bottle of red wine
550ml/1pt lamb or beef stock
1-2 tbsp redcurrant jelly (optional if using lamb stock)

Firstly we need to marinade the lamb. Finely chop or pulse in a processor the salt, rosemary and garlic, making sure you retain some texture. Rub the marinade all over the meat and leave covered in the fridge for 24 hours.

Before tying the lamb, put the duck or goose fat in a roasting tin deep enough for the lamb to be submerged when the fat has melted. Place the tin in a preheated oven at 150-180°C/300-350°F/gas 3-4. Tie the lamb with string to form a neat joint and place in the roasting tin, uncovered. Leave to cook slowly for between 4-5 hours.

When the lamb is cooked it usually floats on the surface of the fat and has a golden colour, and when poked with a fork the juices run clear. It must be remembered that, unlike many lamb dishes, you can not choose to cook the lamb pink and reduce the cooking time because the slow cooking gives the dish its flavour and succulence, as well as rendering most of the fat from the lamb. Carefully remove the lamb from the fat with a carving fork and wrap the lamb fairly tightly in Clingfilm. Leave to cool completely. At this point the lamb can be kept, covered, in the fridge for a number of weeks.

To make the sauce, sauté the garlic, rosemary, carrot and mixed vegetables in a little oil until soft. Pour off the excess oil and add the red wine. Boil until quite syrupy then add the stock and redcurrant jelly, if using. Continue to boil until the sauce coats the back of a spoon. Pass through a sieve.

To serve, slice the lamb (removing the string) into 4 or 5 pieces. Put in an ovenproof dish with some of the sauce to keep it moist, cover with foil and heat in a preheated oven at 170°C/325°F/gas 3 for about 30 minutes.

Meanwhile, make the mash: cook the potatoes in a pan of seasoned water until tender. Tip into a colander to drain. Melt the butter with the herbs and process until well blended. Add to the mash, check the seasoning and keep warm until the lamb is ready.

Spoon a mound of warmed mashed potato into the centre of each plate, place the hot lamb confit on top and pour the sauce over and around the meat. Garnish with rosemary and redcurrants.

Serves 4

Dessert | Whimberry Tart with Lemon Cream

Whimberry is the name given to the wild berries that grow here on the Brecon Beacons and surrounding mountains.The berries have been collected for generations and are enjoyed fresh or cooked into pies and tarts. Whimberies are also known under a range of local names throughout the moorlands of Britain and Europe: bilberry, whortleberry, huckleberry. Their season is very short, just a few weeks in the summer, but if you have the time to scramble around on the mountains it's well worth the effort.

For the Pastry
115g/4oz butter, diced
225g/8oz plain flour
50g/2oz caster sugar
seeds from 1 vanilla pod
50ml/2fl oz milk

For the Lemon Cream
225g/8oz caster sugar
zest and juice of 3 lemons
4 eggs
300g/10oz butter

For the rest of the dish
450g/1lb whimberries
icing sugar, for dusting
3 tbsp water
sprigs of mint, for decoration

To make the pastry, rub the butter into the flour until the mixture resembles breadcrumbs. Stir in the sugar and vanilla seeds then gently work in the milk to form a smooth dough; add a few drops more milk if there are crumbs remaining in the bowl. Wrap in Clingfilm and leave in the fridge for 20 minutes.

Remove the pastry to room temperature a short while before it is required, to let it warm slightly. Grease a 30cm/12" wide by 2.5cm/1" deep, loose-bottomed fluted metal tart tin. Roll out the pastry and use to line the tin, leaving any excess hanging over the sides. Line the pastry case with greaseproof paper and rice or baking beans and bake blind in a preheated oven at 200°C/400°F/gas 6 for 20 minutes. Remove from the oven, take out the paper and baking beans, and cut off the excess pastry with a serrated knife. Slip off the tin ring and leave the tart to cool.

To make the lemon cream, put the sugar and lemon zest in a heatproof bowl over a pan of simmering water for a few minutes to warm the sugar and to infuse the lemon. Whisk the eggs with the lemon juice and add to the bowl of sugar. Stir until the mixture thickens but does not boil. Take off the heat and stir in small amounts of butter at a time. Leave to cool.

Pull the berries gently from their stalks, being careful not to burst the skins. Rinse in a colander and drain. Place in a stainless steel heavy-bottomed pan (do not use aluminium pans). Sprinkle with the sugar and 3 tablespoons of water and bring slowly to the boil. Simmer until the juice is glowing red and the berries have just started to burst their skins. Taste for sweetness (add more sugar if required – but there should be a little tartness). Pour into a heatproof dish and leave to cool.

To serve, carefully pour the lemon cream into the pastry case; it should come halfway up the sides. Spoon the berry mixture on top. Dust lightly with icing sugar and decorate with sprigs of mint.

Serves 8

And...   Red Mullet on Braised Orange and Chilli Fennel

500ml/18floz carton orange juice
300ml/^{1}/$_2$pt white wine vinegar
4 tbsp sugar
2 tbsp sea salt
2 pinches of saffron threads

1 tsp chilli flakes
4 fennel bulbs, cut into
    1.25cm/^{1}/$_2$" slices, feathery
    tops reserved
olive oil, for cooking

salt and pepper
4 x 350g/12oz red mullet,
    filleted, pin-boned and scaled
shredded radicchio, to serve

Mix together the orange juice, wine vinegar, sugar, salt, saffron and chilli flakes. Put the fennel bulbs in a large roasting tin deep enough to cover with the orange juice mix. Cover with foil and cook in a preheated oven at 150°C/300°F/gas 2 for 1 hour. After this time, check that the fennel is tender, if not extend the cooking time.

Pour the cooking liquor into a heavy-bottomed pan and boil over a low heat until it coats the back of a spoon (do not allow it to boil over). At this stage this dressing will be sweet and sour – if preferred, it can be adjusted at this point by adding more sugar or chilli flakes to taste. Meanwhile, keep the fennel warm.

Heat a little olive oil in a non-stick pan. Lightly season both sides of the mullet and cook, skin side down over a high heat for about 2-3 minutes without trying to move the fish. Carefully turn the fish and cook for a further 2-3 minutes.

Place the fennel in the centre of warm plates. Sprinkle with shredded radicchio, and drizzle over the hot saffron and orange dressing. Put the mullet on top and garnish with chopped red chilli (optional) and the reserved fennel feathers.

Serves 4

And...   Beetroot Pesto

Beetroot pesto is ideal to serve with cooked meats, or, as we do, as a garnish for vegetable dishes instead of butter.

450g/1lb raw beetroot (or 2 packets of cooked beetroot)	1 garlic clove, chopped	chopped
300ml/$^1/_2$pt nut oil	50g/2oz Parmesan cheese	salt and pepper
25g/1oz pine kernels	25g/1oz chives, chopped	
	25g/1oz flat leaf parsley,	

Put the beetroot in a pan, cover completely with water, cover the pan and boil gently for about 2 hours. Drain the juice from the beetroot and reserve for later. If using bought beetroot, tip into a colander or sieve and drain well and reserve the juice. Remove the skins and tops and leave the beetroot to cool. (Alternatively, open the packets of cooked beetroot.)

Place the beetroot and half the oil into a food processor and blend finely. Add the pine kernels, garlic and Parmesan and continue to process until smooth. Remove from the processor. Add about 4 tbsp the reserved juice, the chives and parsley, check for seasoning and stir in the rest of the oil.

Serves 4

THE NEW INN AT COLN
Coln St-Aldwyns, Gloucestershire

Brian Evans had been many things before admitting to the madness required to run his own inn; footballer, stockbroker, bistro proprietor, vendor of hotel safes, video producer and husband. He is still a husband and with his wife, Sandra-Anne, he runs one of the leading food inns in the British Isles. On the old Roman Road leading out of Cirencester, in Gloucestershire, the New Inn has been in the forefront of the real pub food revolution since 1992, serving ambitious food in idyllic surroundings. They have a ghost too! Dinner and a good haunting for two is available from a kindly and occasionally visible man in a black cloak, jangling keys! Not ideal for the digestion, perhaps.

Starter | Salad of Ham Hock with Garlic and Parsley

1 bunch of flat leaf parsley
1 ham hock
1 onion, halved
1 carrot, halved lengthways

2 celery sticks
2 bay leaves
1 head of garlic
oil, for cooking

salt and pepper
salad leaves, to serve

Put the parsley stalks (reserve the leaves), ham hock, onion, carrot, celery, bay and garlic (except 2 cloves), in a saucepan, cover with water and bring to the boil. Simmer for 2½-3½ hours. Remove the ham hock, leave until cool enough to handle, then strip the ham from the bone and flake it into small pieces.

Thinly slice the remaining 2 garlic cloves and fry in a little oil until golden but be careful not to take them too far otherwise the garlic will be very bitter. Mix the garlic with the reserved parsley leaves, the flaked ham and the salad leaves. Season and pile on to plates.

Serves 6

Main | Char-grilled Sea Bass with Braised Fennel

For the Braised Fennel
2 fennel bulbs, cut into pieces
butter, for cooking
1 glass of white wine
1 bay leaf

1 star anise
1 glass of chicken stock
salt and pepper

6 x 200g/7oz sea bass fillets
olive oil, for cooking
salt and pepper

To make the braised fennel, seal it in a little butter in a hot pan. When the pieces are evenly coloured, add the wine, bay leaf and star anise, then add the chicken stock and seasoning. Bring to the boil, cover with foil and bake in a preheated oven at 225°C/425°F/gas 7 for 15-20 minutes until you can pierce the fennel with a fork.

Meanwhile, brush the fish with oil and season well. Rub an oven-proof grill pan with oil, heat it then add the fish, in batches, skin side down and cook until the skin is coloured. Transfer to the oven with the fennel for 5 minutes. Serve the fish and fennel together.

Serves 6

Dessert Blancmange with Honey Tuiles and Apricot and Almond Cantucci

For the Cantucci
500g/1lb 2oz caster sugar, plus extra for sprinkling
4 large egg whites
2 tsp vanilla essence
500g/1lb 2oz '00' flour
2 tsp bicarbonate of soda
large pinch of salt
250g/9oz unpeeled almonds
250g/9oz dried apricots, coarsely chopped

1 egg yolk mixed with 2 tbsp milk, to glaze

1 vanilla pod
1.2l/2^1/$_4$pt milk
thinly pared rind of 4 lemons
200g/7oz caster sugar
200g/7oz ground almonds
6 leaves of gelatine, soaked according to the packet instructions

250ml/9fl oz brandy
550ml/1pt double cream, whipped

For the Honey Tuiles
6 large egg whites
25g/1oz honey
250g/9oz icing sugar
250g/9oz plain flour
250g/9oz butter, melted

To make the cantucci, whisk the sugar, eggs and vanilla essence into a creamy mousse then sift in the flour, bicarbonate of soda and salt and fold in gently. Then fold in the almonds and apricots to form a sticky dough. Turn on to a lightly floured surface and shape into sausages 15cm/6" in length, the diameter of a golf ball. Put on a baking tray, brush with the egg yolk glaze and sprinkle with a little sugar. Bake in a preheated oven at 150°C/300°F/gas 2 for 25 minutes until golden and slightly risen. Remove and turn the oven down to low. Cut the 'sausages' in thin biscuits and return to the oven for a further 25 minutes, turning them over halfway through. Cool on a wire rack then store in an airtight container.

To make the tuiles, mix the egg whites with the honey, sugar and flour then slowly pour in the butter, stirring. Leave to rest for 1 hour. Smear the mixture on a large baking sheet. Bake in a preheated oven at 180°C/350°F/gas 4 for about 5 minutes until browned. Remove from the oven and leave to cool before slicing thinly.

To make the blancmange, split the vanilla pod and put it in the milk with the lemon rind. Bring to simmering point then remove from the heat. Add the sugar and ground almonds and leave to infuse for 1 hour. Pour the milk through a fine sieve. The vanilla pod can now be scraped and the seeds added to the lemon-flavoured milk. Put the soaked gelatine in a few tablespoons of the milk and when dissolved add to the milk, followed by the brandy. As the liquid cools it will thicken. Spoon into ramekins and chill until set.

Serves 10

THE NOBODY INN
Doddiscombleigh, Devon

The 16th-century Nobody Inn is set in rolling Devon countryside between the Haldon Hills and the Teign Valley, about six miles from Exeter. Low ceilings, blackened beams, inglenook fireplace, antique furniture and timeless atmosphere retain the unspoilt old-world charm of one of Britain's most famous pubs. The Nobody Inn has long been at the forefront of the real pub food revolution that this innovative cookery book celebrates. Landlord Nick Borst-Smith has built up a formidable reputation over the years for his imaginative wine and whisky list, his extraordinary selection of local cheeses in prime condition and, of course, his wonderful food based on fresh local Devon produce.

Starter   Guinea Fowl Terrine with Dorset Ham

2lb/900g guinea fowl
olive oil, for cooking
salt and pepper
225g/8oz onions, chopped

175g/6oz mushrooms, sliced
225g/8oz butter, chopped
150ml/5fl oz red wine
25g/1oz coriander, chopped

4 slices thinly sliced Denhay
  Farm ham
toast, to serve

Rub the guinea fowl with olive oil and season inside and out. Roast in a preheated oven at 230°C/450°F/gas 8. Leave to cool then strip off and chop the meat.

Fry the onions and mushrooms in the butter until softened. Add the wine and coriander and boil until reduced by half. Add the chopped guinea fowl.

Line a terrine 30 x 10cm/12 x 4" with the ham, leaving enough overhanging the sides to wrap over the top. Pack the guinea fowl mixture into the terrine so that it is overfilled, and press down firmly. Fold the overhanging ham over the guinea fowl mixture. Leave the terrine in the fridge overnight.

To serve, remove the terrine from the fridge in plenty of time. Cut into slices and arrange on serving plates with hot toast.

Serves 4

Main | Roast Salmon with Mediterranean Vegetables

4 x 175-225g/6-8oz pieces of
  salmon fillet, cut from the
  salmon on the diagonal
seasoned flour, for coating
6 tomatoes, cut into chunks
6 cherry tomatoes, cut into
  chunks
2 red and white onions, cut into
  chunks

red, green and yellow peppers,
  cut into chunks
2 sticks celery, cut into chunks
6 mushrooms, cut into chunks
6 gerkins, chopped
12 olives, sliced
sun-dried tomatoes, chopped
$^1/_2$ bottle of dry white wine
15g/$^1/_2$oz basil

15g/$^1/_2$oz oregano
good squeeze of lemon juice
2 tbsp olive oil
salt and pepper
basil, for garnish

Spread the vegetables in a large baking dish. Add the wine, basil, oregano, lemon juice, olive oil and seasoning. Bake in a preheated oven at 220°C/425°F/gas 7 for 30-40 minutes, turning occasionally.

Lightly coat the salmon in seasoned flour and shake off the surplus. Place on a lightly-oiled baking tray and brown under a preheated grill for 3-5 minutes until lightly browned. Then put in the oven below the vegetables for 10 minutes.

To serve, transfer the vegetables to a large dish and put the salmon fillets on top. Garnish with basil.

Serves 4

Dessert | Dark Chocolate Tart

This is good served with a quenelle of mango ice cream.

200g/7oz butter, chopped
250g/9oz plain flour
5 eggs

500g/1lb 2oz plain Belgian
  chocolate, chopped
350ml/12fl oz double cream

200ml/7fl oz milk

Rub the butter into the flour. Add 1 beaten egg and bring together to make a soft dough. Press into a 30cm/12" pastry case and bake blind.

Melt the chocolate in a bain-marie or over a saucepan of hot water. Warm the cream and milk and then add the melted chocolate. Beat the remaining eggs and fold into the chocolate. Gently pour into the pastry case and bake in a low oven at 180-200°C/350-400°F/gas4-6 for about 35 minutes until set.

Serves 4

And...   Venison Braised in Red Wine, with Blackcurrant Compote

We serve the venison with organic vegetables such as yellow, green and black French beans, baby turnips, caramelised shallots, baby onions and three varieties of potato.

1kg/2lb coarsely chopped vegetables – carrot, mushrooms, onion, celery and leek
2 x 225g/8oz venison steaks cut

from the haunch
300ml/$\frac{1}{2}$pt beef stock
$\frac{1}{2}$ bottle of good quality red wine
salt and pepper

225g/8oz blackcurrants
sugar, to taste (optional)

Put the vegetables into a baking tray or ovenproof dish that is at least 7.5cm/3" deep.

Fry or grill the venison steaks on a high heat to seal and colour. Then put on top of the vegetables. Pour over the stock and wine (taste first!). Cover with foil or a well-fitting lid and cook in a preheated oven at 180°C/350°F/gas 4 for 2$\frac{1}{2}$-3 hours.

What to do for 2$\frac{1}{2}$-3 hours? Make the compote from the blackcurrants by heating them in a pan until they burst. Stir and add sugar if necessary. The sauce should be quite tart not sweet.

Remove the cooked and tender venison from the dish and keep warm. Strain the cooking liquor into a pan and boil until reduced and thickened. Season to taste. Put a steak on each plate, cover with the sauce and add a spoonful of compote to the side.

Serves 2

And...   Trout in Filo Pastry with Lemon Sauce

The organic vegetables we serve with the trout are green and yellow courgettes, and Pink Fir potatoes.

3 wild garlic leaves and bulb
115g/4oz butter, plus extra for cooking
1 tsp chopped dried apricot
3 asparagus spears
1 trout weighing about 450g/1lb, filleted

3 sheets filo pastry
1 pinch sesame seeds
lemon slices, to serve

For the Sauce
grated zest and juice of 1 lemon
200ml/7fl oz vegetable stock

12 lemon mint leaves
200ml/7fl oz apple juice
knob of butter
1 egg yolk, beaten
salt and pepper

Make some garlic butter with the wild garlic bulb and the 115g/4oz butter. Add the dried apricot and chill very well. Meanwhile, fry the asparagus in a little butter until tender then leave to cool.

Place the garlic leaves on one of the fillets and the asparagus on top of that. Balance scrapings of garlic butter on top of the asparagus, place the second fillet on top and press down gently.

Carefully put the stuffed trout on to a buttered sheet of filo pastry. Roll the fish up in the pastry and tuck in the sides. Brush with more butter and repeat with sheets two and three. Sprinkle with the sesame seeds. Bake in a preheated oven at 200-220°/400-425°F/gas 6-7 for 15 minutes or until golden brown.

Meanwhile, make the sauce: put the lemon zest and juice into a pan and add the stock, mint and apple juice. Boil for 5 minutes. Remove the pan from the heat, cool slightly then stir a little into the egg yolk along with a knob of butter. Pour this back into the pan and heat very gently, stirring, until thickened; do not allow to boil. Season to taste.

To serve, cut the trout parcel in half with a very sharp knife. Arrange on a plate, pour the sauce onto the side and add some slices of lemon.

Serves 1

And...   Steak and Kidney Pudding

The organic vegetables to accompany this dish include baby courgettes stuffed with chopped Swiss chard, and fondant potatoes.

1 onion, chopped
oil, for cooking
3lbs steak and kidney (approx.
 $^2/_3$ braising steak and $^1/_3$
 kidneys)

200ml/7fl oz bitter beer
200ml/7fl oz vegetable stock
salt and pepper

For the Pastry
175g/6oz fresh breadcrumbs
75g/3oz plain flour
50g/2oz suet
1 egg, beaten

Fry the onion in a little oil in a saucepan or flameproof casserole until softened and coloured. Add the meat and again fry until coloured. Pour in the beer, stock and seasoning, cover the pot and simmer for about 3 hours until tender.

Meanwhile, make the pastry: mix all the ingredients with 1 $^1/_2$ tbsp water and knead to make a dough. Leave to rest for 1 hour.

Drain the meat and leave to cool. Retain the juice. Line a pudding basin with two thirds of the pastry. Fill with the meat mixture. Use the remaining pastry to make a lid to fit on top. Cover the top of the pudding basin with a pleated piece of greaseproof paper. Put in a steaming basket above a saucepan of simmering water, cover the steamer and steam for 45 minutes.

Boil the reserved meat juices until thickened to make a sauce.

To serve, carefully invert the pudding on to a warmed plate, pour over some of the sauce and serve piping hot accompanied by the remaining sauce

Serves 6

And...	Tomato, Ginger and Whisky Chutney

Excellent served with the Guinea Fowl Terrine (see page 94).

115ml/4fl oz red wine vinegar
115g/4oz soft brown sugar
12 tomatoes, chopped

2 onion, finely diced
50g/2oz fresh root ginger,
 chopped

1 tot of whisky, to taste

Put the vinegar and brown sugar in a small non-aluminium pan and boil until reduced to less than half.

Add the tomatoes, onion and ginger. Cook over a low heat for 2 hours, stirring frequently to prevent sticking, until there is no free liquid.

Purée half the chutney in a blender. Then add back to the remaining half. Add whisky to taste. Store in a kilner jar until required.

Makes 450g/1lb

THE PEAR TREE
Whitley, Wiltshire

Historically The Pear Tree was a farmstead built in 1750 but when present owners, Martin and Debbie Still, took over in 1997 they set about turning it into one of the most exciting pubs for food in Britain. Locally sourced fresh produce with an emphasis on simplicity and clarity of flavours mark out the style of the kitchen. Set in four acres of parkland, with pear trees used to mark the former monastic boundaries, The Pear Tree Inn has achieved great things in a relatively short time. Even greater things seem set to follow.

Starter	Beetroot, Roast Hazelnut and Feta Roulade

1.5kg/3lb beetroot
250g/9oz hazelnuts, browned,
  skinned and coarsely crushed
250g/9oz feta cheese, grated
50ml/2fl oz hazelnut oil

For the Vinaigrette
500ml/18fl oz orange juice
75ml/3fl oz white wine vinegar
1 tsp Dijon mustard
1 tbsp clear honey

For the rest of the dish
1 tbsp egg yolk
300ml/$^1/_2$pt virgin olive oil
salt and pepper
$^1/_2$ bunch chives, chopped

Place the beetroot in a roasting tin and cover with water. Cover the tin with foil and bake in a preheated oven at 200°C/400°F/gas 6 for about 1 hour until tender. Leave to cool in the liquid then skin the beetroot and slice finely, preferably on a mandolin.

Spread the hazelnuts on a sheet of Clingfilm about 20cm/8" square. Top with the sliced beetroot followed by the feta and seasoning. Drizzle over the hazelnut oil. Roll up the Clingfilm carefully, pulling tightly along the way. Tie the ends and leave for 24 hours.

To make the vinaigrette, boil the orange juice until reduced to 35ml/1$^1/_2$fl oz. Put in a food processor with the other ingredients except the oil and chives. Blend together and slowly pour in the oil until the dressing emulsifies. Add the chives just before serving.

Slice the roulade in the Clingfilm to required size, then tip it on its side and cut off the Clingfilm. Garnish with mixed leaves and serve with the orange and chive vinaigrette.

Serves 8

Main — Corn-fed Chicken with Celeriac and Vanilla Gratin and Grilled Figs

For the Gratin
1 head celeriac, very thinly sliced
4 large baking potatoes, very
 thinly sliced
2 vanilla pods
300ml/$\frac{1}{2}$pint double cream
300ml/$\frac{1}{2}$pint milk

1 tbsp celery salt
black pepper

For the Balsamic Reduction
100ml/3$\frac{1}{2}$fl oz balsamic
 vinegar
100ml/3$\frac{1}{2}$fl oz red wine

100g/3$\frac{1}{2}$oz caster sugar

8 corn-fed boneless chicken
 breasts
8 figs, halved
rosemary sprigs

For the gratin: lay the celeriac slices in a deep roasting tin and put the potatoes on top. Split the vanilla pods, remove the seeds then mix with the remaining ingredients and pour over the celeriac and potatoes. Cover with a sheet of greaseproof paper and bake in a preheated oven at 180°C/350°F/gas 4 for about an hour until the potatoes are tender, the cream has reduced and it has set quite firm. You may decide to serve the gratin immediately. However, we bake it in advance, then cut circles from it and reheat in plain ring cutters.

For the balsamic reduction, place all ingredients in a saucepan and reduce by half – this should be syrupy but sharp enough to cut through the richness of the gratin.

Seal the breasts and then roast in a preheated oven at 200-220°/400-425°F/gas 6-7 for 15-20 minutes, until the juices run clear when tested with the point of a knife.

Grill the figs until tender, then spear with the rosemary sprigs, if liked.

To serve, put a portion of gratin on a plate, drizzle the balsamic reduction around the plate, cut the chicken in half on an angle. Sit the chicken on top of the gratin and garnish with the grilled figs speared with rosemary.

Serves 8

Dessert — Coffee and Cardamom Ice Cream in a Tuile Basket with Rum Syrup

The ice cream recipes makes 1.75l/3pt.

550ml/1pt milk
550ml/1pt double cream
15g/$\frac{1}{2}$oz cardamom pods
50g/2oz freshly ground coffee
12 egg yolks
300g/10oz caster sugar

For the Tuile Baskets
3 small egg whites
185g/6$\frac{1}{2}$oz icing sugar
15g/$\frac{1}{2}$oz plain flour
125g/4$\frac{1}{2}$oz melted butter

For the Rum Syrup
25ml/1fl oz dark rum
50g/2oz caster sugar

Pour the milk and cream into a saucepan, add the cardamom pods and coffee and bring to the boil.

Whisk the egg yolks and sugar until stiff.

Strain the milk and cream through a fine sieve and whisk slowly into the egg mixture. Leave to cool and churn in an ice-cream machine according to the manufacturer's instructions. Transfer to a freezer-proof container and put in the freezer. Alternatively, put the mixture in a freezer-proof container and freeze until set around the edges. Tip into a bowl and beat to break up the ice crystals. Return to the container then the freezer. Repeat twice more, then freeze until firm.

To make the tuile baskets, mix all the ingredients together to form a smooth paste. Place spoonfuls, spaced well apart, on large baking sheets, spread out and bake, in batches, if necessary, at 200°C/400°F/gas 6 until golden. While still warm, mould over an oiled small bowl or ramekin and leave to cool and set. Carefully ease the tuiles off the moulds, and store in an airtight container.

To make the syrup, boil the dark rum with the sugar for about 10 minutes until syrupy. Leave to cool.

To serve, scoop balls of ice cream into the baskets and drizzle syrup around the plates. Garnish with red berries and shaved bitter chocolate

Serves 12

And... Raspberry, Lime and Ricotta Cheesecake

250g/9oz butter, melted
250g/9oz ginger nut biscuits, crushed
250g/9oz ground almonds
500g/18oz cream cheese
500g/18oz ricotta cheese

6 eggs
200g/7oz caster sugar
200g/7oz soured cream
grated zest and juice of 6 limes
2 tbsp cornflour mixed with 2 tbsp water

500g/18oz fresh or frozen raspberries
clotted cream and lightly sweetened raspberry purée, to serve

Line a 25cm/10" springform cake tin with greaseproof paper. Mix the butter with the biscuits and ground almonds. Press into the base of the tin.

Put all remaining ingredients except 250g/9oz of the raspberries into a mixer and whisk to combine. Pour on to the base, then drop the remaining raspberries on top. Bake at 150°C/300°F/gas 3 for about 40 minutes until golden and a knife comes out clean from the centre. Leave to cool then carefully remove from the tin. Serve a wedge of cheesecake with a spoonful of clotted cream and the raspberry purée.

Serves 16

And...	Focaccia Bread

Delicious cut in slices and dipped in olive oil or cut in half and filled with your favourite sandwich mix.

150ml/5fl oz olive oil, plus extra
   for brushing
300ml/^{1}/$_2$pt boiling water
1^1/$_2$ tsp caster sugar
75g/3oz fresh yeast, crumbled

550ml/1pt cold water
1.3kg/3lb strong bread flour
^{1}/$_2$ tbsp mixed herbs
^{1}/$_2$ tbsp tsp pesto
^{1}/$_2$ tbsp chopped sun-dried

tomatoes
^{1}/$_2$ tbsp salt
rock salt and chopped rosemary,
   for sprinkling

Mix the olive oil, boiling water and sugar with 550ml/1pt cold water, add the yeast and leave in a warm place until a froth forms on the surface.

Put the flour, herbs, pesto, sun-dried tomatoes and salt in a mixer with a hook attachment, or a food processor. Add the wet mix and knead for 15 minutes, or according to the manufacturer's instructions. If you do not have a mixer, knead the dough by hand but it's painful! Stand the bowl in a warm place and cover with a clean tea towel. Leave to double in size.

Remove the dough from the bowl to a floured surface and knock back the dough to expel the air. Divide the mixture into 175g/6oz balls. Roll out the balls into oval-shaped breads about 2cm/^{3}/$_4$" thick, place on to baking sheets, brush liberally with olive oil and make holes in the top with your fingers, or the floured handle of a wooden spoon.

Leave in a warm place to prove for 10 minutes then bake in a preheated oven at 220°C/425°F/gas 7 for about 20-25 minutes. After 5 minutes open the oven and sprinkle over some rock salt and chopped rosemary. The focaccia are ready if they sound hollow when tapped underneath.

Makes 12

THE PELICAN
All Saints Road, London W11

Opened in 2001 in Ladbroke Grove, The Pelican is the third and youngest of the three organic pubs owned by Esther Boulton and Geetie Singh that have created such a stir in the world of real pub food (see page 34 for The Crown and page 38 for The Duke of Cambridge). You will find the same style of simple, European influenced dishes here as you would in The Pelican's sister pubs. Food cooked with great skill, full of flavour, served in relaxed, comfortable, stripped-back surroundings, based on the finest organic ingredients available.

Starter	Broad Bean, Feta, Olive, Cumin and Mint Salad

1.5kg/3lb 6oz large broad beans; or 500g/1lb 2oz young sweet broad beans
350g/12oz feta cheese, crumbled

handful of Kalamata olives
handful of mint leaves

For the Dressing
100ml/3^1/$_2$fl oz extra virgin olive oil
1^1/$_2$ tsp cumin seeds
2 garlic cloves, finely chopped
juice of 2 lemons
salt and pepper

If using large broad beans, add to a pan of boiling water, quickly return to the boil and cook for 5 minutes. Drain, leave until cool enough to handle then squeeze each bean so that the tender inside pops out of its skin. Leave to cool completely. If using small young beans, cook them in boiling salted water for a few minutes, drain and leave to cool.

To make the dressing, heat the olive oil over a low heat, add the cumin seeds and garlic. Continue to heat until the garlic just begins to change colour. Take off the heat and pour into another container to cool and prevent the garlic browning further. When cool, whisk in the lemon juice and season to taste.

To serve, toss the broad beans, feta, olives and mint leaves in a bowl with the dressing. Leave for a few minutes for the flavours to develop.

Serves 6

Main | Fish Stew with Saffron, Chilli, Red Peppers, Potato and Coriander

250g/9oz mussels
250g/9oz clams
6 tbsp extra virgin olive oil
1 large onion, halved and sliced
  lengthways
3 cloves garlic, thinly sliced
2 bay leaves

pinch of saffron filaments
2 red chillies, split in half
2 red peppers, chopped
4 potatoes, cut into wedges
150ml/5fl oz white wine
1 x 225g/8oz can chopped
  tomatoes

150ml/5fl oz fish stock
salt and pepper
750g/1^{3}/₄lb monkfish fillet, cut
  into chunks
chopped coriander, to serve

Rinse the mussels and clams and discard any open ones that do not close when tapped on a work surface.

In a large saucepan, heat the olive oil then add the onion, garlic and bay leaves. Cook over a low heat until softened. Stir in the saffron, chillies, peppers and potatoes, cover and cook slowly until the peppers are soft. Turn up the heat, add the white wine and cook until reduced. Then add the tomatoes and fish stock. Season and cook until potatoes are soft. Add the monkfish, cook for 2-3 minutes then add the mussels and clams. Cook until all the mussels and clams are open, discarding any that don't open. Add chopped coriander and check the seasoning then spoon into warmed bowls.

Serves 6

Dessert   Citrus Cake

This cake is best made 24 hours in advance.

200g/7oz sugar
100g/3½oz ground almonds
50g/2oz fresh breadcrumbs
1 tsp baking powder
zest of 1 orange
zest of 2 lemons

200ml/7fl oz vegetable oil
4 large eggs

For the Syrup
75g/3oz golden caster sugar
juice of 1 orange

juice of 3 lemons
5 star anise
1 cinnamon stick
5 cardamom pods, lightly
   crushed

Combine all the dry ingredients in a bowl. Mix the oil and eggs in a separate bowl then stir into the dry ingredients to make a runnyish batter.

Grease a 23cm/9" springform cake tin and line with baking parchment. Pour in the cake mixture and bake in a preheated oven at 190°C/375°F/gas 5 for 20 minutes. Then cover with a sheet of moistened, crumpled baking parchment and bake for a further 30 minutes.

Meanwhile, make the syrup: put all the ingredients in a saucepan and heat gently until the sugar has melted. Increase the heat and boil for 5 minutes.

Strain the syrup over the cake as soon as it comes out of the oven. Leave the cake to cool in the tin before turning out.

Serves 8-10

And...   Pan-fried Sea Bass with Leek and Tarragon Risotto

For the Risotto
2 leeks, halved lengthways and
   sliced
115g/4oz unsalted butter, plus
   extra for cooking
1 onion, finely chopped
2 garlic cloves, chopped
2 celery sticks, finely chopped
500g/1lb 2oz arborio rice

150ml/5fl oz white wine
1.75l/3pt fish stock
250g/9oz crème fraîche
2 bay leaves
2 stalks of tarragon, chopped

juice of 2 lemons
50ml/2fl oz olive oil, plus extra
   for frying

salt and pepper
4 x 175g/6oz sea bass fillets,
   skin side scored with a sharp
   knife

To make the risotto, cook the green parts of the leeks in a little butter and then set aside.

Cook the onion, garlic and celery with a little salt and the bay leaf in 50g/2oz of the butter in a saucepan. Halfway through add the white parts of the leek. When the vegetables are soft, add the rice. Stir until all the rice is coated in vegetables and butter, then add the wine. Boil until it has reduced. Start to stir in the hot stock, a ladle at a time, stirring continuously until each ladleful has been absorbed. Continue for about 15 minutes until the rice is almost cooked, then beat in the rest of the butter, the tarragon and crème fraîche and finally the green parts opf the leek.

Meanwhile, whisk the lemon juice, 50ml/2fl oz olive oil and seasoning together. Set aside.

Heat the olive oil in a frying pan. Season the sea bass fillets and fry for 2-3 minute on each side until golden brown. Serve the fish on top of the risotto with a little of the lemon oil poured over.

Serves 6

And... Slow-cooked Shoulder of Lamb

1 lamb shoulder, 2kg/4-5lb, boned, fat removed and cut into 3cm/1$\frac{1}{4}$" chunks
1 tsp dried oregano
zest and juice of 2 lemons

5 tbsp extra virgin olive oil
2 onions, halved and sliced lengthways
2 bay leaves

seasoning
2l/3$\frac{1}{2}$ pt lamb stock

Toss the chunks of lamb in oregano, lemon zest and half the olive oil. Cover with Clingfilm and refrigerate overnight.

Heat the remaining olive oil over a medium heat and add the onions and bay leaves. Turn the heat down and cook gently for 15 minutes. Remove the onions and increase the heat. Season the lamb and add to the oil in batches. Cook each batch until brown, remove and add next batch.

Return the onion and lamb to the pan, add the lamb stock and lemon juice, ensuring all the lamb is covered with liquid. Cover and cook slowly for 1$\frac{1}{2}$-2 hours until the meat is tender. Remove from the heat and leave to cool before chilling for several hours.

The lamb can be reheated on the stove or wrapped, with crumbled feta cheese on top, in foil parcels then baked in a preheated oven at 180-190°C/350-375°F/gas 4-5 for 30 minutes.

Serves 8

THE PENHELIG ARMS
Aberdyfi, Gwynedd

A delightful 16th-century inn with a wonderful setting overlooking the Dyfi estuary, serving excellent real pub food which in fine weather can be taken by the sea wall. Run by Robert and Sally Hughes – Robert does the cooking and Sally is front of house – it has built up a fine reputation as one of the leading dining pubs in the country. Menus are based on daily-supplied local fish, with meat and vegetables from local producers and traders who are also loyal and enthusiastic customers.

Starter	**Warm Goats' Cheese Salad**

115g/4oz lean smoked bacon, diced
4 small slices of white bread, diced
1 small log of goats' cheese (not too hard), cut into 1.2cm/½" slices

2 tbsp seasoned flour
1 egg, beaten
2 tbsp white breadcrumbs
4 tbsp good olive oil
1 tbsp wine vinegar
1 tsp Dijon mustard

a few salad leaves, and black olives, to serve

Spread the bacon and bread in a shallow ovenproof dish and bake in a preheated oven at 190°C/375°F/gas 5, stirring occasionally, until golden brown.

Roll the goats' cheese slices in the seasoned flour to coat evenly, then dip into the egg. Allow the excess to drain off before rolling the slices in the breadcrumbs. Lay in a shallow ovenproof dish and bake in the oven for 5-8 minutes until golden.

Put the oil, vinegar, mustard and salt and pepper in a screw-top jar and shake vigorously to make a vinaigrette.

Toss the salad leaves in some of the vinaigrette and pile on to plates. Place the cheese carefully on top. Scatter over the crisp bacon, croutons and olives, drizzle with a little more vinaigrette and serve.

Serves 2

| **Main** | **Fillet of Cod Grilled with Tomatoes, Capers, Anchovies and Mozzarella** |

2 x 175g/6oz cod fillets
olive oil
chopped coriander, parsley and
  chives
garlic purée

4 tomatoes, peeled, deseeded
  and chopped
1 tbsp good capers, rinsed and
  drained
a few anchovy fillets

1 x 150g/5oz mozzarella
  cheese, sliced
coriander leaves and diced red
  pepper, to garnish

Coat the cod fillets in olive oil, coriander, parsley, chives and garlic and cook under a preheated grill for 8-10 minutes, depending on the the thickness and size, until the flesh flakes easily.

Mix the tomatoes, capers and anchovies together and place on top of the fish. Cover with thin slices of cheese and continue to grill until the cheese is golden.

Serve the fish with the cooking juices spooned over and garnished with coriander leaves and finely diced red pepper.

Serves 2

| **Dessert** | **Pears in Warm Fudge Sauce with Vanilla Ice Cream** |

175g/6oz granulated sugar
2 ripe pears
150ml/5fl oz double cream

115g/4oz butter
150g/5oz soft brown sugar
pinch of ground ginger

few drops of vanilla essence
vanilla ice cream, to serve

Make a syrup by dissolving the granulated sugar in 50ml/2fl oz water over a low heat and then increasing the heat until the syrup boils. Boil for a few minutes, turn down the heat and add the pears. Poach for about 10-15 minutes until tender.

Meanwhile, make the fudge sauce by gently heating the cream, butter, brown sugar and ground ginger over a low heat until the sugar has dissolved. Bring to the boil and immediately remove from the heat. Add a few drops of vanilla essence to taste.

Slice the pears in half and take out the cores. Lay the halves on plates with scoops of vanilla ice cream and pour over the warm fudge sauce.

Serves 2

QUEEN'S HEAD HOTEL
Troutbeck, Cumbria

This wonderful and historic 17th-century coaching inn on the old Windermere to Penrith route has a terrific national reputation for imaginative food served in picturesque surroundings. You can dine in the Mayor's parlour, the venue for Troutbeck's traditional mayor making ceremony or enjoy great bar food at a bar converted from a massive Elizabethan four-poster bed.

Starter	Home-cured Salmon and Hot-smoked Salmon in Filo Pastry

If you don't possess a smoker then buy good quality Scottish smoked salmon.

For the Cured Salmon
225g/8oz fresh salmon
2 tsp sugar
2 tsp sea salt
dill, enough to coat
$1\frac{1}{2}$ tbsp brandy

For the Smoked Salmon
225g/8oz fresh salmon
2 bay leaves
salt and pepper

For the Dressing
$1\frac{1}{2}$ tbsp honey
3 tbsp lemon juice

$1\frac{1}{2}$ tbsp white wine
1 tsp English mustard
350ml/12fl oz olive oil

filo pastry
oil, for frying

To make the cured salmon, lay a sheet of Clingfilm on a plate, and put the salmon on the Clingfilm. Sprinkle the sugar and salt over the salmon then top with the dill. Sprinkle over the brandy. Wrap the salmon in the Clingfilm, put another plate on top and weight it down. Leave in the fridge for about 24 hours.

Meanwhile, make the smoked salmon: make deep cuts in the salmon and put in a hot smoking cabinet. Season with bay leaves and salt and pepper. Put the cooker on the stove and cook for 15-20 minutes. Leave to cool.

To make the dressing, mix the honey, lemon juice, wine and mustard together. Slowly pour in the oil, whisking to make an emulsified dressing. Season to taste.

To assemble the dish, cut 7.5cm/3" rounds from the filo pastry (you need 3 per portion) then fry in oil until golden. Drain on paper towels. Slice the cured salmon very thinly. Flake the smoked salmon. Alternate the two salmons between filo pastry rounds and place the stacks in the centre of each plate. Drizzle the dressing around the outside.

Serves 4

Main — Braised Lamb Shanks with Rosemary and Redcurrant Jus

4 lamb shanks,
  450-675g/1-1$\frac{1}{2}$lb each
seasoned flour
oil, for cooking
1 *mirepoix* e.g. 1 carrot, 1 onion,
  1 leek and 1 garlic clove,
  finely chopped
$\frac{1}{2}$ bottle of red wine

2 tbsp redcurrant jelly
few sprigs rosemary
2 tbsp tomato purée
mashed potato flavoured with
  mint, to serve
sprigs of rosemary and
  redcurrants, to garnish

For the Rosemary and Redcurrant Jus
1 *mirepoix* of vegetables
2 tbsp redcurrant jelly
2 tbsp tomato purée
2 sprigs rosemary
salt and pepper

Roll the shanks in plenty of seasoned flour then fry in hot oil to seal the outside. Spread the vegetables in a roasting tin and put the shanks on top. Pour in the wine and add the jelly, tomato purée and rosemary. Add water to cover the meat then cover the tin with foil. Cook in a preheated oven at 220°C/ 425°F/gas 7 for 2-2$\frac{1}{2}$ hours until the meat is just falling off the bone. Remove the shanks and keep warm. At this stage, the shanks can be left to cool then refrigerated, covered, if liked. Then, to serve, put the shanks in a roasting tin they just fit, add water to come about one third of the way up, cover with foil and put in an oven preheated to 220°C/425°F/gas 7 for about 20 minutes.

To make the jus, remove the fat from the top of the lamb-shank stock to a pan and use for frying the vegetables until brown. Add the wine and boil until reduced by half. Then spoon in the redcurrant jelly and tomato purée and add the rosemary. Return to the boil and add the lamb stock. Simmer until reduced to a thick sauce. Pour through a fine sieve. Season to taste.

Serve the shanks on minted mashed potatoes with the jus poured over. Garnish with sprigs of rosemary and redcurrants.

Serves 4-6

Dessert | Bread and Butter Pudding with Apricot Glaze and Crème Anglaise

1kg/2lb loaf, preferably Fruit and Stout Bread (see page 113), thinly sliced, crusts removed
6 eggs, whisked
425ml/15fl oz double cream
150ml/5fl oz milk
75g/3oz soft dark brown sugar

50g/2oz sultanas

For the Crème Anglaise
2 egg yolks
40g/1$\frac{1}{2}$oz vanilla sugar
300ml/$\frac{1}{2}$pt double cream

For the Apricot Glaze
1 x approx 350g/12oz jar apricot jam
25g/1oz caster sugar

Cut each slice of bread in half diagonally.

Whisk the eggs with the cream, milk and half the sugar.

Lay a layer of bread in an ovenproof dish, then sprinkle over some of the remaining sugar and some of the sultanas. Pour over some of the egg mixture. Continue in this way until all the bread and egg mixture have been used. Sprinkle the remaining sugar over the top. Bake in a preheated oven at 170°C/325°F/gas 3 for 30-35 minutes until set. You may like to put a tray of water in the bottom of the oven to help to keep the pudding light and moist.

Meanwhile, make the crème anglaise: cream the egg yolks with the sugar. Warm the cream in a heavy-bottomed pan then stir into the egg mixture. Pour back into the pan and heat very gently, stirring continuously, until the sauce coats the back of the spoon; do not allow to boil.

To make the apricot glaze, put the jam and sugar in a pan with 150ml/5fl oz of water. Stir, bring to the boil and simmer for 5 minutes.

To serve, spoon a pool of crème anglaise on to each warm plate, place a portion of the pudding in the middle of the plate and pour some of the glaze over the top.

Serves 6-8

And...   Fruit and Stout Bread

35g/1½oz fresh yeast
pinch of sugar
300ml/½pt Murphy's stout, at
  blood heat

565g/1lb 4oz coarse brown flour
salt
35g/1½oz unsalted butter, or
  lard

1 egg yolk
1 tbsp dark treacle
50g/2oz sultanas

Cream the yeast with the sugar, then stir in a little of the stout. Leave for about 10-15 minutes until frothy.

Mix the flour and salt together then rub in the butter or lard. Gradually stir in the yeast liquid and remaining stout, the egg yolk, treacle and sultanas to make a smooth dough. Knead well for about 15 minutes until firm and elastic. Form into a ball, put into an oiled bowl and turn the dough over so that it is covered in oil. Cover with a damp cloth and leave in a warm place until doubled in volume.

Turn the dough onto a lightly floured work surface and knead for 5 minutes. Form into a loaf shape and put into an oiled 1kg/2lb loaf tin. Cover and return to the warm place until the dough has risen to just above the top of the tin.

Bake in an oven preheated to 200°C/400°F/gas 6 for 20-25 minutes; to test if the loaf is cooked, remove it from the tin and tap the bottom of the loaf – if it sounds hollow it is ready. Leave to cool on a wire rack.

Makes 1 x 1kg/2lb loaf

THE RED LION
Burnsall, North Yorkshire

Situated on the banks of the river Wharfe in the heart of beautiful Wharfedale, this 16th-century ferrymans' inn has been dispensing hospitality for the last 300 years. Surrounded by the fells and large estates of the Yorkshire Dales the food reflects the wealth of local meat, game and produce available to Head Chef Jim Rowley. Beef, lamb and pork are reared specially for the pub by local farmers. Game - grouse, partridge, pheasant and venison - is bought in by local estates, while much of the veg comes straight form the local farm.

Starter	Blue Wensleydale Mousseline

1 x 175g/6oz chicken breast, chopped	75g/3oz blue Wensleydale cheese	salt and pepper
2 egg whites	75ml/3fl oz whipping cream	1 leek, cut into strips and blanched

Put the chicken and egg whites into a blender and mix together. Add the cheese, cream and seasoning and whizz briefly, just to incorporate the cream. (Do not overmix otherwise the cream will 'split'.)

Line 6 ramekins with Clingfilm, leaving an overhang all round. Then line with the leek strips, again allowing them to overhang the edge. Fill the ramekins with the cheese mixture and fold over the leeks and Clingfilm. Steam for about 10 minutes until slightly risen and firm to the touch. Unwrap the Clingfilm and turn the mousselines on to warmed plates.

Serves 6

Main	Pot Roast Gloucester Old Spot Pork

Ask the butcher to French-trim the rib bones, and remove the skin from the loin, but to leave the fat on.

1x 2kg/4lb rib end loin of Gloucester Old Spot, chined	2 onions, chopped	vegetable stock, see method
4-6 garlic cloves, sliced	1 head of celery, chopped	apple sauce and slices of grilled dry-cured smoked bacon, to
rosemary sprigs	1 carrot, chopped	serve
	1 bulb of garlic, cut in half	

Criss-cross the fat and pierce the pork fat with a sharp knife and insert the whole garlic cloves and the rosemary sprigs.

Spread the chopped vegetables and the garlic bulb in a roasting tin so that they cover the bottom of the roasting tray and put the pork on top. Pour in 5cm/2" of vegetable stock and cook uncovered in a preheated oven at 180°C/350°F/gas 4 for 3 hours until meltingly tender. Top up the liquid as necessary. Transfer the pork to a rack and leave to rest in a warm place for 10-15 minutes.

Strain the stock into a jug, leave to stand then skim off all the fat.

Carve the pork between the bones into mini joints and serve with the strained stock, apple sauce and a slice of grilled smoked bacon on top.

Serves 8

Dessert | Posh Bananas and Custard with Caramel

For the Pastry
1 egg
1 egg yolk
75g/3oz icing sugar
115g/4oz butter, slightly
  softened
300g/10oz plain flour

For the Banana Mix
50g/2oz butter
4-5 bananas, diced
25ml/1fl oz dark rum
25g/1oz brown sugar

For the Custard
4 egg yolks

50g/2oz caster sugar
550ml/1pt whipping cream

For the Caramel Sauce
115g/4oz caster sugar
50ml/2fl oz water
115ml/4fl oz double cream

To make the pastry, mix the egg, egg yolk and icing sugar together. Work in the butter, using a wooden spoon then add the flour. Gently form into a dough using your fingertips; do not overmix. Roll into a ball, cover with Clingfilm and leave in the fridge for at least 1 hour.

Use the pastry to line 6 loose-bottomed individual tartlet tins. Bake blind in a preheated oven at 180°C/350°F/gas 4 for 10 minutes; do not allow to brown. Leave to cool.

Meanwhile, to make the banana mix, melt the butter in a non-stick frying pan, add the bananas, rum and sugar. Cook over a high heat for 2-3 minutes until caramelised. Quickly remove the mixture from the pan to stop further cooking. Leave to cool.

To make the custard, beat the egg yolks and sugar together. Warm the cream to blood heat and beat into the egg mixture.

Divide the banana mixture among the tartlet cases. Pour over the custard. Return to the oven for 15-20 minutes until the custard is set.

Remove the tartlets from the tins onto warm plates.

To make the caramel sauce, gently heat the sugar in 50ml/2fl oz water, stirring until dissolved. Boil until the syrup becomes a mid-brown caramel. Remove from the heat and, using a long-handled whisk to avoid being splashed, carefully whisk in the cream. Drizzle around the tartlets.

Serves 6

And... Fillets of Sea Bass with Celeriac Mash and Green Tomato Chutney

For the Chutney
1/2 onion, finely chopped
1 garlic clove, finely chopped
olive oil, for cooking
4 courgettes, cut into
  1cm/1/2" dice
3-4 beef tomatoes, peeled,
deseeded and chopped
115ml/4fl oz white wine vinegar
115g/4oz sugar

1kg/2lb celeriac, chopped
175g/6oz butter
salt and pepper

6 x 350g/12oz sea bass, scaled
  and filleted
seasoned flour
pesto and balsamic vinegar, to
  serve

To make the chutney, fry the onion and garlic in a little olive oil until soft. Add the courgettes, fry for 2-3 minutes then add the tomatoes vinegar and sugar. Boil rapidly for 5-10 minutes until thick. Keep warm.

Meanwhile, steam the celeriac until tender. Put into a blender with the butter and seasoning and purée until smooth.

Coat the sea bass fillets in seasoned flour and fry in olive oil for about 4 minutes on each side until lightly browned and cooked through.

To serve, spoon a mound of celeriac mash in to the centre of 6 warmed plates, and circle with pesto and balsamic vinegar. Put 2 sea bass fillets across each mound and top with warm chutney.

Serves 6

And...   Spinach, Wild Mushroom and Cambazola Canneloni

For the Sauce
8 plum tomatoes, chopped
1 onion, chopped
1 fennel bulb, chopped
5 garlic cloves, chopped
olive oil, for cooking 1l/1³/₄pt

tomato juice
6 sun-dried tomatoes, chopped
handful of basil
salt and pepper

450g/1lb wild mushrooms
450g/1lb spinach
115g/4oz garlic butter
450g/1lb Cambazola
24 fresh lasagne sheets

To make the sauce, cook the tomatoes, onion, fennel and garlic in a little olive oil until soft. Add the tomato juice and simmer for 20 minutes. Stir in the sun-dried tomatoes and cook for a further 10 minutes. Add the basil and seasoning and pulse to a rough consistency with a hand blender.

Meanwhile, cook the mushrooms and spinach separately in the garlic butter. Leave to cool.

Cut the cheese into 2.5cm/1" long strips the same width as the lasagne sheets.

Blanch the lasagne in hot water for 30 seconds. Drain and lay them flat. Put a cheese strip across the width. Divide the mushrooms and spinach among the sheets and roll up tightly. Put, join side down, in 1 large or 6 individual gratin dishes. Pour over the sauce and bake in a preheated oven at 180°C/350°F/gas 4 for 10-15 minutes.

Serves 6

RIVERSIDE INN
Aymestrey, Herefordshire

Close to the Mortimer Trail, between Ludlow and Kington, Steve and Val Bowen's beautiful Riverside Inn stands on the banks of the trout rich, gurgling River Lugg. The chefs at The Riverside wisely make use of the fantastic local produce available, with top quality meat from the Welsh Marches, and vegetables, salads and herbs from their own gardens. Everything you would hope for in a country pub: log fires, antique furniture, a rambling beamed-bar, fine ales and wines and, most important of all, as far as this book is concerned, great food.

Starter | Warm Salad of Lobster and Pâté de Foie Gras

1 x 450g/1lb live lobster
1.2l/2pt court bouillon
3 tbsp lardons
5 tsp hazelnut oil
3 tbsp croutons

2-3 tbsp raspberry vinegar
1 shallot, finely chopped
25g/1oz unsalted butter
150-175g/5-6oz
    pâté de foie gras

salad of radicchio, curly endive, sweetcorn and cherry tomatoes, and pine kernels, to serve

Cook the lobster in the court bouillon for about 10 minutes. Keep it warm in the liquid.

Fry the lardons in the hazelnut oil until crisp. Add the croutons and fry, remove from oil, wrap in paper towel and keep warm.

Stir the vinegar and shallots into the pan sediment and bring to the boil. Whisk in the butter, a piece at a time. Keep warm.

Remove the lobster from the shell.

Toss the salad ingredients in warm dressing and arrange on 6 plates. Top with lobster, foie gras, lardons and croutons and sprinkle finely with pine kernels. Serve immediately.

Serves 6

Main | Aymestrey Pheasant with Chestnuts

1 tbsp olive oil
25g/1oz butter
1 cock pheasant, jointed
2 onions, sliced
225g/8oz peeled chestnuts

2 tablespoons flour
425ml/15fl oz meat stock
150ml/5fl oz claret (plus a glass
    to drink whilst cooking)
115g/ 4oz fresh cranberries

grated rind and juice of 1 orange
salt and pepper
root vegetables and game chips, to serve

Heat the oil and butter together in a frying pan and brown the pheasant for a few minutes. Transfer to an ovenproof casserole.

Fry the onions and chestnuts in the frying pan; add more oil and butter if necessary. Remove and add to the pheasant.

Stir the flour into the remaining fat, then stir in the stock and wine to make a smooth sauce. Bring slowly to the boil, still stirring, and when it thickens, pour over the pheasant. Add the cranberries, orange rind and juice and season to taste. Cover and cook in a preheated oven at 180°C/350°F/gas 4 for about 1 hour until tender.

Serve with fresh root vegetables and game chips.

Serves 4

Dessert | Pancakes with Raspberry Coulis

300g/10oz fresh raspberries
  (or blackberries, if available)

115g/4oz icing sugar, sifted
juice of 1 lemon

4 pancakes to your own recipe
4 berries, for decoration

About 1 hour before you make your pancakes, prepare the coulis: put all the ingredients in a blender and blend together. Add more sugar or lemon as required; the coulis should be a little on the sharp side to complement the pancakes. Strain through a fine sieve and chill in the fridge until required.

Serve around each pancake and top with 1 fresh berry.

Serves 4

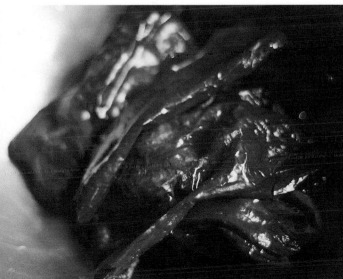

THE ROEBUCK INN
Brimfield, Herefordshire

The Roebuck Inn had a very distinguished previous life as a quite formal restaurant with bars before David and Sue Lloyd-Wilson took it over in 1997 and decided to turn it into a more relaxed country pub. The emphasis is still on serving wonderful food and it helps their cause being close to the gastronomic heartland of Ludlow with its gang of Michelin starred restaurants. David Lloyd-Wilson oversees the kitchens which produce imaginative and robustly flavoured dishes drawing on the wonderful local produce available from the Welsh Marches.

Starter	Gin-soused, Home-cured Fillet of Salmon with Dill Dressing

We have chosen this dish because it is one of our most popular starters. It is a variation of gravadlax and more interesting than smoked salmon. It is easily made and should provide an impressive start to a dinner party, a tasty filling for sandwiches and rolls for a picnic, or as a topping for canapés if chopped and mixed with fromage frais.

For the Gin 'Cure'
6 tbsp coarse salt
6 tsp black peppercorns
1 bay leaf
2 tsp juniper berries
3 tbsp caster sugar

1kg/2lb piece fresh salmon, skin on, trimmed and pin-boned (the fishmonger should do this for you – if not, change him)
gin
good handful finely chopped dill

For the Dressing
15ml/6fl oz soured cream
75g/3oz caster sugar
4 tbsp cider vinegar
about 1 tbsp chopped dill

mixed salad leaves, to serve
thin slices of dill pickles or cucumber, to serve (optional)

To make the 'cure', grind the ingredients together in a coffee blender, spice grinder or pestle and mortar. Spread half the mixture in a shallow dish or tray that is large enough to hold the salmon and has been lined with Clingfilm. Put the salmon on the cure, skin side down. Cover with the remaining 'cure'. Rub it in and ensure that it is well covered. Splash a good amount of gin over the fish. (We use our home-made damson gin.) Cover tightly with Clingfilm, put a weight on top and put in the fridge. Turn twice a day for two or three days.

Unwrap the salmon and swill off the 'cure' under a cold tap. Pat dry with paper kitchen towels.

Lay the salmon, skin side down, on a large piece of Clingfilm. Pat the dill over the salmon. Wrap in Clingfilm until required.

To make the dressing, mix all the ingredients together.

To serve, slice the salmon as thinly as possible with a sharp, thin-bladed knife, and arrange neatly around a serving plate. Put a pile of mixed salad leaves in the centre and drizzle the dressing around the salmon slices.

Serves 6

Main	Breast of Guinea Fowl Stuffed with a Confit of its Legs

3 guinea fowl
2 tbsp sea salt
1 bunch of thyme
1 tbsp black peppercorns

2 bay leaves
1kg/2lb rendered duck fat
  (available from a good butcher
  with a bit of notice)

15g/$\frac{1}{2}$oz chopped herbs such
  as parsley and chervil
oil, for cooking

Take the breasts off the guinea fowl, keeping the skin intact. Remove the legs and put in a shallow dish. Sprinkle with sea salt, cover and leave in the fridge overnight. Remove from the dish, rinse off the salt and pat dry.

Put the legs, thyme, peppercorns and bay leaves into a pan so that they just fit easily. Cover with duck fat and poach in a very low oven for about 3 hours until very tender and falling off the bone. Cool in the fat. Remove the skin from the legs and shred the meat with a fork into a bowl. Add salt and pepper, the herbs and a little of the fat to bind the mixture together. Cover and chill. Store the remaining fat in a jar in the fridge for another time.

Make a neat incision lengthways in the skin of each guinea fowl breast to form a pocket and fill with the leg mixture. Seal with a cocktail stick or two. Fry quickly, skin side down, in a little oil to brown and crisp the skin then transfer to a preheated oven at 180°C/350°F/gas 4 for 15–20 minutes. Leave to rest for 5 minutes before carving neatly on to the serving plate.

Serves 6

Dessert	Iced Fruit Crumble

For the Apple Crisps
150g/5oz caster sugar
50ml/2fl oz water
1 apple, peeled and cored
lemon juice

For the Ice Cream
1 vanilla pod, split

550ml/1pt whole milk
1 egg yolk
1oz/25g caster sugar
300ml/$\frac{1}{2}$pt double cream
150ml/5fl oz apple purée
50ml/2fl oz Calvados
50ml/2fl oz blackberry purée
50ml/2fl oz crème de mure

For the Crumble Mixture
225g/8oz plain flour
75g/3oz butter
150g/5oz demerara sugar
25g/1oz ground almonds

To make the apple crisps, gently heat the sugar in 50ml/2fl oz water until dissolved then bring to the boil. Leave to cool. Slice the apple very thinly, ideally with a mandolin. Dip in lemon juice and then in the sugar syrup. Arrange on silicon paper and place in the bottom of a very cool oven for about 2 hours until dry.

To make the ice cream, scrape the seeds from the vanilla into the milk. Add the pod and bring the milk to the boil.

Meanwhile, whisk the egg yolks and sugar together in a bowl sitting over, not in, a saucepan of simmering water, until rich and creamy. Add the milk and whisk over the saucepan until a smooth custard is formed. Remove the bowl from the pan, cover with a clean cloth and allow to cool. Lift out the vanilla pod and add the double cream to the custard. Put in the fridge.

Flavour the apple purée with Calvados and the blackberry purée with crème de mure: the liqueurs act as an 'anti-freeze' so the cream does not set too hard.

Mix all the ingredients of the crumble together, spread in a baking tray and bake in a preheated oven at 180°C/350°F/gas 4 for 20 minutes, stirring occasionally. Remove and leave to cool.

To assemble, divide the cream mixture in half. Churn one half in an ice-cream machine. Alternatively, pour one half of the mixture into a freezer-proof container, freeze until beginning to set around the edges then tip into a bowl and beat to break up the ice crystals; do not allow to melt. Return to the container and then the freezer. Repeat once more. Just before the mixture sets, add one of the purées and stir together.

Line 8 metal rings with silicon paper to form a collar about 7.5cm/3" high, and place on a sheet of silicon paper on a flat tray. Divide the ice cream evenly among the lined rings, top with some of the crumble mix and press down into the ice cream. Freeze on a level surface.

Repeat the ice cream making process with the other half of the mixture, adding the purée as before. Divide among the half-filled rings. Top with the crumble mix and return to the freezer to finish setting.

Remove from the freezer 5 minutes before serving to allow to thaw slightly. Pour a little of the fruit coulis around each plate, place the crumble in the centre; remove the ring and the silicon paper. Garnish with apple crisps and dust with icing sugar.

Serves 8

And...　　　Hazelnut Biscotti

100g/3$\frac{1}{2}$oz shelled hazelnuts, blanched	$\frac{1}{2}$ tsp baking powder	2 large eggs, beaten
175g/6oz plain flour	175g/6oz golden caster sugar	1 tsp vanilla essence
	pinch of salt	

Spread the nuts on a baking tray and roast in a preheated oven at 180°C/350°F/gas 4 for 10 minutes until browned.

Sift the flour and baking powder into a bowl and stir in the sugar and salt. Make a well in the centre and add the eggs and vanilla essence.

Form into long sausage lengths about 2.5cm/1" wide on silicone paper on a baking sheet. Space the 'sausages' about 7.5cm/3" apart because they spread during baking. Bake for 25 minutes then allow to cool before slicing diagonally into 1.2cm/$\frac{1}{2}$" slices. Return to the switched-off oven for about 1 hour to dry. Store in an airtight container. Serve with strong coffee or vin santo.

Makes about 75-100 small biscuits

And... | Crab Filo Parcels

Mini parcels can also be made to serve as canapés or a pre-starter.

150g/5oz finely diced shallot
2 tsp crushed garlic
100g/3½oz diced celery
100g/3½oz butter, plus extra for brushing
4 tbsp Worcestershire sauce

3 tbsp tomato purée
3 tbsp Madras curry paste
100g/3½oz plain flour
550ml/1pt milk, warmed
500g/1lb 2oz crab, half white and half brown meat

juice of 1 lemon
25g/1oz coriander
salt and pepper
12 x 30cm/12" sheets of filo pastry

Cook the shallots, garlic and celery in the butter over a low heat until soft. Add the Worcestershire sauce, tomato purée and curry paste. Cook briefly then stir in the flour to make a roux. Cook for a few minutes then slowly pour in the warmed milk, stirring constantly. Bring to the boil, whisking, to form a thick sauce.

Cool slightly before carefully stirring in the crab so as not to break up its texture. Add the lemon juice, coriander and seasoning to taste. Leave until cold.

Cut a sheet of filo into 4 squares. Brush with butter and place them, overlapping diagonally, on top of each other. Put a small amount of crab filling in the centre and then bunch up the edges of the filo and twist slightly to form a seal. The parcels should be about the size of a walnut. Brush with melted butter. Repeat with the remaining pastry and filling. The parcels can be made up to this stage in advance and kept in the fridge until required.

Bake the parcels in a preheated oven at 180°C/350°F/gas 4 for about 10 minutes until light golden brown and crisp. Serve with dressed mixed salad leaves, lime wedges and a light tomato or pepper dressing.

Makes 48 walnut sized parcels

And... | The Roebuck House Dressing

5 shallots, chopped
2 garlic cloves, chopped
1 tbsp demerara sugar
2 tbsp Dijon mustard

2 tbsp wholegrain mustard
250ml/9fl oz olive oil
115ml/4fl oz sunflower oil
115ml/4fl oz cider vinegar

lemon juice, to taste
salt and pepper

Mix the shallots, garlic, sugar and mustards in a blender then slowly pour in the oils and vinegar. Add lemon juice and salt and pepper, to taste.

Makes about 700ml/1¼pt

THE ROYAL OAK
Yattendon, Berkshire

This extremely handsome and stylish 16th-century country inn, in the centre of the beautiful Berkshire village of Yattendon, serves food of the highest quality to an enthusiastic following. This is a serious kitchen that takes pride and considerable trouble to produce dishes that emphasise natural flavours and textures. Log fires and fresh flowers inside and a delightful garden for fine weather dining just add to the experience.

Starter — Onion and Cider Soup

6 large white onions, sliced
3 garlic cloves
olive oil, for cooking
115g/4oz butter, diced

4 cooking apples, peeled, cored
 and sliced
250ml/9fl oz dry cider
1.7l/3pt chicken stock

550ml/1pt double cream
salt and pepper
snipped chives and croutons, to
 serve

Cook the onions and garlic in a little olive oil and the butter in a heavy-bottomed pan, for 10 minutes; do not brown. Add the apples and cider and simmer until reduced. Add the chicken stock and cream and simmer for about 30 minutes. Cool slightly, then purée in a food processor. Pass through a fine sieve.

Return the soup to the pan and bring back to the boil. Season and serve garnished with snipped chives and croutons.

Serves 6

Main — Slow-roasted Belly of Pork with Oyster Sauce and Sweet Potato Confit

2kg/4lb belly of pork, the skin
 scored
2 tsp Chinese five spice powder
salt and pepper
50ml/2fl oz sesame oil
1 large red chilli, chopped

1 tbsp grated root ginger
6 heads green pak choi
8 tsp oyster sauce

For the Sweet Potato Confit
1kg/2lb sweet potatoes, diced

olive oil, for cooking
2 garlic cloves, peeled
1/2 bunch of coriander, chopped
1 red chilli, chopped
salt and pepper

Put the pork belly in a roasting tray and sprinkle the fat side with the Chinese five spice and salt and pepper. Pour a little sesame oil over and bake in a preheated oven at 170°C/325°F/gas 3 for 3 hours. Slice before serving.

Meanwhile, make the sweet potato confit: put the sweet potatoes in a pan and cover with olive oil. Add the garlic and cook slowly until the potatoes are tender. Drain off the oil before serving. Sprinkle over the coriander, chilli and seasoning.

Heat a wok and add the chilli and ginger and cook for 2 minutes. Then add the pak choi and oyster sauce and cook for 5 minutes only. Tip into a large serving dish. Arrange the sweet potatoes around and finish with the sliced belly pork and crisp crackling.

Serves 6

Dessert | Lemon Posset

For the Posset
850ml/1$\frac{1}{2}$pt double cream
250g/9oz caster sugar
juice of 3 lemons

For the Raspberry Coulis
1kg/2lb raspberries, puréed
200g/7oz icing sugar
2 tsp lemon juice

For the rest of the dish
strawberries and sprigs of mint, to decorate

Bring all the ingredients for the posset to the boil and simmer for a few minutes. Leave to cool slightly, then pour into glasses. Cool completely and place in the fridge until set.

To make the coulis, gently simmer all ingredients together than pass through a fine sieve. Cool before chilling.

To serve, pour some of the raspberry coulis on top of each glass of posset and decorate with strawberries and a sprig of mint.

Serves 6

And... | Spicy Thai Fish Cakes with Tomato Jam

For the Tomato Jam
500g/1lb 2oz ripe plum
  tomatoes
3 red chillies, deseeded and
  chopped
3 garlic cloves, chopped
2 knobs of root ginger, chopped
300g/10oz caster sugar

100ml/3$\frac{1}{2}$fl oz red wine vinegar

1kg/2lb of mixed fish, such as
  salmon, cod and tuna,
  chopped
2 egg whites
2 tbsp Thai red curry paste
juice of 2 limes

2 tsp cornflour
salt
1 bunch of spring onions,
  chopped
1 bunch of coriander, chopped
oil, for deep frying
rocket salad, to serve

To make the tomato jam, purée all the ingredients in a blender, then pour into a heavy-bottomed pan (not aluminium) and simmer, stirring as necessary to prevent sticking, until all the liquid has gone, like chutney. Transfer to a sterilised jar.

Process the fish in a food processor until smooth then add the egg whites, curry paste, lime juice and cornflour. Transfer to a bowl and add the spring onions and coriander. Roll the fish mixture into small balls. Half-fill a deep pan with oil and heat to 180°C/350°F. Add the fish balls in batches and fry for 5-6 minutes, until golden. Drain on paper towels and keep warm while frying the remaining balls. Serve hot with the tomato jam and a rocket salad.

Serves 6

And... Smoked Haddock Kedgeree

For the Curry Cream Sauce
225g/8oz chopped shallots
100ml/3½fl oz white wine
  vinegar
500ml/18fl oz white wine
1l/1¾pt double cream
2 tbsp mild curry paste
juice of 1 lemon

salt, to taste

500g/1lb 2oz long grain white
  rice
200g/7oz button mushrooms,
  sliced
oil, for cooking
4 hard-boiled eggs, chopped

1 bunch of dill, chopped
1kg/2lb smoked haddock
200ml/7fl oz double cream
salt and pepper
6 eggs
chopped chives, to serve

To make the sauce, put the shallots in a pan with the white wine vinegar and reduce slowly until all the vinegar has gone. Add the white wine and reduce by two thirds then add the cream and reduce by one third. Whisk in the curry paste, lemon juice and a little salt. Simmer for 5 minutes then pass through a sieve. Bring back to the boil to serve.

Meanwhile, boil the rice for about 15 minutes or according to the instructions on the packet, until tender. Refresh in cold water, drain and place to one side.

Meanwhile, fry the button mushrooms in the oil until soft. Add to the rice with the hard-boiled eggs and dill.

Gently poach the haddock in the cream for 7-10 minutes. Once cooked, add to the rice and mix everything together. Season to taste. Place the mixture in small moulds and steam for 10 minutes, or microwave for 5 minutes.

Poach the eggs in a pan of barely simmering water until cooked to your liking.

Turn the rice moulds on to warmed plates. Lift the poached eggs from the water with a fish slice, drain briefly and put on the rice mounds. Cover with the curried cream sauce. Finish with chopped chives.

Serves 6

And...	**Bitter Chocolate Tart**

For the Pastry
225g/8oz plain flour
100g/3$^{1}/_{2}$oz icing sugar
100g/3$^{1}/_{2}$oz butter
1 egg, beaten
1$^{1}/_{2}$fl oz water

For the Filling
350ml/12fl oz double cream
200ml/7fl oz milk
500g/1lb 2oz good quality plain
   chocolate, chopped
3 eggs, beaten

To Serve
chocolate shavings and a sprig
   of mint, to decorate
clotted cream

Sift the flour and icing sugar together into a bowl then beat in the butter, egg and 1$^{1}/_{2}$fl oz water until the pastry is smooth. Leave to rest in the fridge for 30 minutes.

Line a 25cm/10" tart tin evenly with the pastry and place in the fridge for a further 10 minutes. Bake blind in an oven preheated to 170°C/325°F/gas 3 for 10 minutes and then leave on a wire rack to cool.

To make the filling, boil the cream and milk. Add the chocolate and then the eggs. Mix for 1 minute. Slowly pass through a fine sieve. Pour the mixture into the pastry case and bake at 170°C/325°F/gas 3 for 5 minutes until the tart has a glossy finish.

Leave to cool before decorating with chocolate shavings and a sprig of fresh mint, and serving with clotted cream.

Serves 8

SEAFOOD BAR & RESTAURANT
St Monans, Fife

Tim Butler's stunning Seafood Bar and Restaurant, overlooking the Isle of May and Bass Rock, is one of Scotland's finest. The bar is still a bar and anyone and everyone is welcome to pop in for a drink, but the heart of the place is the excellent restaurant. By using locally sourced produce from the natural larder of Scotland and its seas, lochs and lands, The Seafood Restaurant gives no excuse to its customers not to return.

Starter | Pan-seared Scallops with Herb Risotto and Thai Coconut Sauce

For the Orange Reduction
1l/1^{3}/$_{4}$pt orange juice
2 vanilla pods
10 cardamom pods, crushed
2 garlic cloves
250ml/9fl oz balsamic vinegar

For the Thai Coconut Sauce
25g/1oz root ginger, coarsely chopped
1 shallot, chopped
4 lemon grass stalks, coarsely chopped

2 garlic cloves, chopped
1 small red chilli, deseeded and chopped
1^{1}/$_{2}$ tbsp olive oil
1 can coconut milk
a few drops of Thai fish sauce
50g/2oz brown sugar
1 tbsp lime juice
50ml/2fl oz double cream

1 shallot, chopped
olive oil for cooking
200g/7oz arborio rice

1l/1^{3}/$_{4}$pt chicken stock
1 small aubergine
1l/1^{3}/$_{4}$pt vegetable oil
8 small asparagus spears, preferably Thai - use the top 5cm/2"
50ml/2fl oz double cream
salt and pepper
1 tbsp chopped parsley
8 king scallops, halved horizontally
small knob of butter

To make the orange reduction, boil the orange juice, vanilla pods, cardamom, garlic and balsamic vinegar until reduced to 150ml/5fl oz. Strain and leave to cool.

To make the Thai coconut sauce, cook the ginger, shallot, lemon grass, garlic and chilli in the olive oil over a low heat until the shallot is soft. Add the coconut milk, Thai fish sauce, sugar, lime juice and cream and simmer for 15-20 minutes. Strain and keep warm.

Meanwhile, in a saucepan, cook the shallot in a little oil over a low heat until tender. Add the rice, brown slightly then pour in the chicken stock a little at a time; allow the liquid to be absorbed before adding any more. Leave to simmer for 10-12 minutes until the rice is tender. Strain and refresh under running cold water.

Peel the aubergine and cut the skin into fine strips. Heat the vegetable oil to 190°C/375°F in a deep pan. Deep fry the aubergine skins for 1-2 minutes until crisp; use the aubergine for another dish. Drain on kitchen paper then season with a little salt.

Cook the asparagus in boiling salted water for 2-4 minutes, depending on size, until just tender. Drain well.

To serve, place the rice in a pan with the cream, season to taste and heat through. Add the parsley and divide among 4 heated plates. Put 2 asparagus tips on each risotto. Sear the scallops in hot butter for 20 seconds on either side. Add 4 halves to each plate. Spoon Thai coconut sauce and orange reduction around the plate and top with the aubergine.

Serves 4

Main	**Roast Breast of Pigeon with Ravioli of Leg Confit and Red Onion Marmalade**

In the restaurant discs of potatoes, cooked in stock and then brushed with butter and finished in the oven, and butter beans cooked in chicken stock, and carrots cooked in water, butter and sugar, also accompany this dish.

2 squab pigeons
1 tbsp rock salt
Chinese five spice powder
$^1/_2$ orange, sliced
2 garlic cloves
2 sprigs of tarragon
2 sprigs of thyme
1 small tin of goose fat
1 carrot, chopped
1 onion, chopped
2 celery sticks, chopped
oil, for cooking

$^1/_2$ bottle red wine
55ml/1pt brown chicken stock

For the Red Onion Marmalade
2 red onions, sliced
oil, for cooking
50g/2oz brown sugar
2$^1/_2$ tbsp red wine vinegar

For the Savoy Cabbage
$^1/_2$ Savoy cabbage, divided into

leaves
100g/3$^1/_2$oz smoked streaky bacon, diced
50g/2oz pine kernels, toasted
75ml/3fl oz double cream

For the Ravioli
50g/2oz shiitake mushrooms, sliced
butter, for cooking
8 won ton skins
beaten egg

Remove the breasts from the squab and set aside. Remove the legs and sprinkle with rock salt, place in a small casserole dish and dust with Chinese five spice powder, add the orange, garlic, tarragon and thyme and cover with the goose fat. Cover and cook in a preheated oven at 140°c /275°f gas mark 1 for 2 hours.

Meanwhile, chop the squab carcasses, put in a roasting tin and add the carrot, onion and celery and a little oil. Fry until browned then add the red wine and bring to the boil, stirring to dislodge the sediment. Tip into a large saucepan, add the brown chicken stock, bring to the boil, skim then boil until reduced by two thirds.

To make the marmalade, cook the onions in a little oil over a low heat heat until tender. Add sugar and vinegar and reduce until syrupy. Set aside and keep warm.

Remove the central stalks from the cabbage and blanch the leaves in boiling salted water for 1 minute. Drain and refresh in cold water. Drain again. Finely shred the cabbage. Dice the bacon and cook in a little oil in a pan over a low heat. Add the pine kernels, cabbage and cream and simmer until the cream has thickened. Set aside and keep warm.

Drain the squab legs, remove the meat from the bones and chop finely. Cook the mushrooms in butter until soft then add them to the chopped meat. Spread one quarter of the mixture on one won ton skin, leaving a border around the edge. Brush with beaten egg then cover with another skin and brush the edges together to seal. Repeat with the remaining skins and filling.

Sear the squab breasts on both sides, season and place in a preheated oven at 220°C/425°F/gas 7 for 5-6 minutes, or until cooked to your taste. Remove and leave to rest in a warm place.

Strain the stock into another pan and reduce further until almost syrupy.

To serve, divide the cabbage and marmalade between 4 warmed plates. Put the ravioli on the cabbage. Slice the squab and arrange on the marmalade, and pour the sauce around the plate.

Serves 4

Dessert — Prune and Armagnac Puddings with Banana and Ice Cream

For the Ice Cream
6 egg yolks
115g/4oz caster sugar
2 bananas
500ml/18fl oz milk
2 vanilla pods, split
250ml/9fl oz double cream, whipped

For the Sesame Florentines
115g/4oz caster sugar
50ml/2fl oz double cream
50g/2oz sesame seeds
75g/3oz glucose syrup

For the Prune and Armagnac Puddings
75g/3oz prunes (pitted and pre-soaked)
$1/2$ tsp bicarbonate of soda
75ml/3fl oz water
$1^1/2$ tbsp Armagnac
75g/3oz brown sugar
25g/1oz butter, softened
1 egg, beaten
100g/$3^1/2$oz self-raising flour
$1/2$ tsp baking powder

For the Sauce
50g/2oz caster sugar
50g/2oz unsalted butter
juice of $1/2$ lemon
50ml/2fl oz double cream

For the Fruit salad
75ml/3 floz stock syrup
75ml/3fl oz water
$1/2$ pineapple, diced
$1/2$ mango, diced
$1/2$ banana, sliced

To make the ice cream, whisk the egg yolks and sugar until thick and pale and the whisk leaves a trail when lifted.

Purée the bananas in a blender with a little of the milk, then transfer to a saucepan with the remaining milk and the vanilla pods. Bring to the boil and pour into the egg mixture, stirring. Return to the pan and heat gently, stirring constantly, to form a custard; do not allow to boil. Pour through a sieve into a bowl, cover the surface with Clingfilm and leave to cool before putting in the fridge.

When the custard is cold, fold in the whipped cream. Churn in an ice-cream machine, or pour into a shallow freezer-proof container and put in the freezer until beginning to set. Spoon into a cold bowl and beat to break up the ice crystals but do not allow to melt. Return to the container and put in the freezer. Repeat once then leave to freeze completely.

To make the sesame florentines, put all the ingredients into a saucepan, bring to the boil and stir continuously for 1 minute. Spread the mixture on a silicon-paper-lined baking sheet. When heated the mixture will spread out and should be quite thin. Bake in a preheated oven at 180°C/350°F/gas 4 for about 5-6 minutes until golden brown.

Remove from the oven and place a second silicon sheet on top. Roll the mixture until it is thin. Cut into four 18 x 3cm/7 x 2¼" strips and roll around a mould such as a pastry cutter to form a shape. Leave to cool and set aside.

To make the puddings, put the prunes and bicarbonate of soda into a saucepan with 75ml/3fl oz water and bring to the boil. Add the Armagnac and purée briefly in a blender. Leave to cool.

Cream the sugar and butter until light. Beat in the egg, prune purée, flour and baking powder. Spoon into 4 greased small timbales (or cup-shaped moulds) so they are half-filled. Bake in a preheated oven at 170°C/325°F/gas 3 for 15-20 minutes.

To make the sauce, put the sugar and butter in a pan and bring to the boil, whisking, until it starts to caramelise. Take off the heat, stir in lemon juice and cream and keep warm in a bain-marie

To prepare the fruit, dissolve the sugar in 75ml/3fl oz water over a low heat then bring to the boil. Add the pineapple. Simmer until it starts to become soft then add the mango and banana to warm through.

To serve, unmould the puddings on to 4 warmed plates and coat with sauce. Stand a florentine upright and place a ball of ice cream in the centre. Spoon the warm fruit salad around the plate.

Serves 4

And... Half a Dozen Grilled Kilbrandon Oysters with Creamed Leeks

6 rock oysters, preferably Kilbrandon, Isle of Seil
1 leek, white part only, finely shredded
1 shallot, finely chopped
olive oil, for cooking
50ml/2fl oz dry white wine
double cream
salt and pepper

Shuck the oysters and drain off the sea-water.

In a pan, cook the leek and shallot in a little olive oil over a low heat until tender. Add the wine and cream and reduce until almost dry. Season to taste; beware – the oysters are quite salty. Spoon the creamed leeks on to the oysters in their shell, and put under a preheated grill until the top is golden brown. Serve carefully.

Serves 2

And... Grilled Fillet of Turbot with Basil Dressing and Herb Potatoes

For the Basil Dressing
50g/2oz basil
50ml/2fl oz white wine vinegar
25g/1oz sugar
1 tbsp French mustard
250ml/9fl oz olive oil

For the Herb Potatoes
1kg/2lb Desirée potatoes
15g/$^1/_2$oz basil, finely chopped
15g/$^1/_2$oz tarragon, finely chopped
15g/$^1/_2$oz chives, finely chopped
50ml/2fl oz balsamic vinegar
2 tbsp sugar
3 tbsp wholegrain mustard
250ml/9fl oz olive oil

For the rest of the dish
1 red pepper, halved
1 yellow pepper, halved
1 green pepper, halved
olive oil, for cooking
2 pinches of rubbed thyme
1 pinch of rock salt
1 bunch of asparagus, trimmed and halved
1kg/2lb turbot, filleted and skinned, or 4 large fillets, skinned
12 cherry tomatoes
250g/9oz shiitake mushrooms, sliced
1 pinch of blackened Cajun spices
chopped herbs, for garnish (optional)

To make the basil dressing, put the basil leaves, vinegar, sugar and mustard in a blender and mix together. Slowly pour in the oil to emulsify the dressing. Season and transfer to a bottle for pouring.

To make the herb potatoes, cook the potatoes in boiling water until soft. Drain and leave to cool in cold water. Drain again then roughly crush by hand. Add the herbs and salt. Whisk the vinegar, mustard and sugar together then slowly add the olive oil. Add to the potatoes and mix thoroughly.

Lay the peppers, skin side up, in a baking tray or shallow baking dish and drizzle olive oil over. Sprinkle over the thyme and rock salt. Roast in a preheated oven at 220°C/425°F/gas 7 for 30 minutes until the skins have blistered; take out of the oven and cool. When cold, skin and slice thinly. Pour the oil into a large sauté pan or frying pan and reserve.

Cook the asparagus in boiling salted water for about 5-7 minutes until tender. Cool under cold running water and drain well. Separate the tips from the stalks. Slice the stalks diagonally and put to the side.

Reheat the potatoes.

Meanwhile, cut each fish fillet in half diagonally, and season the skin side; this will be the presentation side. Heat a large frying pan, add a little olive oil and when it is smoking lay the fish, presentation side down in the oil and sear for 30 seconds. Add a few drops of oil on top of the fish. Next add in the cherry tomatoes to the pan and toss the pan so the tomatoes are coated in oil. This will soften them and allow them to take colour. Place the pan under a preheated grill for about 6 minutes, turning the fish half way through until it is quite spongy to touch; be careful not to overcook.

Heat the pan of pepper cooking oil, add the mushrooms and fry for 3-5 minutes until softened. Add the peppers and sliced asparagus stalks, season and add a large pinch of Cajun spice. Add the asparagus spears and toss until piping hot.

Divide the potatoes among 4 warmed plates. Spoon some of the vegetables over and around the potatoes. Place a piece of turbot on top of the vegetables on the potatoes, add more vegetables and place final piece of fish on top. Drizzle basil dressing around the plate. Place 3 cherry tomatoes in a triangle on each plate and lean an asparagus spear against each cherry tomato. Garnish with herbs, if liked, and serve.

Serves 4

THE SPREAD EAGLE
Sawley, Lancashire

Famous for many years as one of the leaders in the real pub food movement The Spread Eagle continues to blaze a trail through the culinary consciousness of Lancastrians and devotees from further afield. On the banks of the River Ribble with panoramic views of the Ribble Valley the kitchen here produces dishes influenced by the great European brasserie-style of cooking.

Starter	Grilled Black Pudding with Mash and Mustard Sauce

1kg/2lb floury potatoes, quartered
1 bunch of spring onions, chopped
1 leek, white part only, chopped
115ml/4fl oz milk
butter

salt, pepper and freshly grated nutmeg
4 x 2oz pieces of black pudding cut from a black pudding stick

For the Mustard Sauce
4 shallots finely chopped

butter or oil, for cooking
150ml/5fl oz chicken stock
300ml/$\frac{1}{2}$pt double cream
1 tbsp wholegrain mustard
1 tsp smooth Dijon mustard

Boil the potatoes in seasoned water until tender. Add the spring onions and leek to a pan, cover with the milk and bring to the boil. Drain the potatoes and mash with a fork or put through a ricer. Gradually beat in the milk mixture until smooth. Add the butter and season with salt and pepper and nutmeg.

Meanwhile, make the mustard sauce: cook the shallots in a small amount of butter or oil, over a low heat until soft. Next add the chicken stock and reduce by half, add the cream and reduce by one third. Whisk in the mustard, season and keep warm.

To serve, brush each piece of black pudding with butter and place under a medium grill until hot. Divide the potato mixture among 4 hot soup plates, placing it in the centre. Pour the mustard sauce around it and place a piece of black pudding on the potato.

Serves 4

Main	**Slow-cooked Duck Legs with Herb Crumb and White Bean Casserole**

8 duck legs
250g/9oz sea salt
1 large sprig of thyme
1 sprig of rosemary
1 head of garlic, split
750g/1¾lb duck or goose fat
4 bay leaves

For the Bean Casserole
1 onion, diced

2 celery sticks, diced
2 large carrots, diced
4 garlic cloves, finely chopped
olive oil, for cooking
250g/9oz haricot beans, soaked
 overnight and drained
600ml/1pt 2fl oz chicken stock
4 tomatoes, chopped
1 tsp thyme flowers
1 tsp chopped basil

For the Herb Breadcrumbs
4 slices day-old bread, crusts
 removed
2 garlic cloves
4 tbsp chopped parsley
salt and pepper
50g/2oz butter, melted and
 cooled

Trim all the excess skin and fat from the duck legs to obtain a neat shape. Score around the drumstick and remove the knuckle end with a heavy sharp knife so as not to split the bone. Place the legs into a shallow dish and cover with the sea salt. Put into the fridge and leave for 6 hours. Preheat the oven to 150°C/300°F/gas 2, remove the duck legs from the salt, rinse and pat dry. Place the legs into a large pan, add the herbs and garlic and melted duck fat and place on a medium heat until it comes to a gentle simmer, then cook in a preheated oven at 170°C/320°F/gas 3 for 2½ hours until the meat comes easily away from the bone. Leave to cool then drain off the fat.

Meanwhile, make the bean casserole: heat a little olive oil in a thick-bottomed pan, add the onion, celery and carrots and sweat until soft. Add the garlic and cook for a further 2 minutes then stir in the beans and stock. Simmer for about 2 hours or until the beans are soft. Stir in the tomatoes and herbs, cook for 2 minutes then remove from heat.

To make the herb breadcrumbs, put the bread, garlic, parsley and seasoning into a food processor and mix together. Add the butter to give a mixture that resembles green breadcrumbs which hold together when squashed.

To serve, heat the duck legs in a moderate oven until hot and slightly crispy. Meanwhile, divide the hot bean mixture between 4 deep main course bowls, place 2 hot duck legs in each of the bowls on top of the bean casserole, sprinkle with the herb crumb and place under a hot grill for 30 seconds.

Serves 5

Dessert | Vanilla and Rosewater Burnt Cream with Dried Fruit Compote

For the Fruit Compote
4 apple slices, diced
1 tbsp sultanas
1 tbsp dried cranberries
8 large prunes
8 dried apricots
1 stick cinnamon
300g/10oz caster sugar
300ml/$^{1}/_{2}$ pt water

For the Sesame Tuiles
150g/5oz sesame seeds
150g/5oz icing sugar
150g/5oz plain flour
40ml/1$^{1}/_{2}$fl oz orange juice
100g/3$^{1}/_{2}$oz unsalted butter,
   melted

For the rest of the dish
8 egg yolks
50g/2oz caster sugar
35ml/1$^{1}/_{2}$fl oz rose water
425ml/15fl oz double cream
1 vanilla pod
icing sugar, for glazing

To make the dried fruit compote, the night before the compote is required you need to soak the fruits together in water.

The next day, dissolve the sugar in 300ml/$^{1}/_{2}$pt water in a large saucepan over a low heat, stirring. Boil for 1 minute without stirring. Drain the fruits and add to the pan with the cinnamon stick. Poach for about 30 minutes. Leave to cool.

To make the sesame tuiles, mix all the dry ingredients together, then add the orange juice and butter and beat until smooth. Place tablespoonfuls of the mixture on non-stick baking trays and spread evenly with a pallet knife which has been dipped in hot water, to obtain discs. Bake in a preheated oven at 180°C/350°F/gas 4 for 6-8 minutes until golden brown. Leave to cool slightly before removing and moulding into shape around a rolling pin. Store in an airtight container.

Put the egg yolks, sugar and rosewater in a bowl and mix well with a whisk. Pour the cream into a saucepan. Scrape the seeds from the vanilla pod into the cream, add the pod and bring to the boil. Pour the hot cream over the egg mixture and mix well. Leave to cool and press through a fine sieve.

Divide the mixture among 4 medium ramekin dishes and put them in a small roasting tin. Pour boiling water around the dishes and cook in a preheated oven at 170°C/325°F/gas 3 for 35-40 minutes until the mixture is just soft. Leave to cool.

To serve, dust the cooked creams heavily with icing sugar, and caramelise under a preheated hot grill until golden. Place on 4 large plates and spoon the fruit compote next to them. Finish with a crisp tuile.

Serves 4

And...   Chicken Liver and Wild Mushroom Parfait

250g/9oz wild mushrooms, puréed
115ml/4fl oz red wine
1 sprig of thyme
2 garlic cloves, split

2 shallots, diced
450g/1lb butter, plus extra for cooking
450g/1lb chicken livers
2 tsp salt

1 tsp white pepper
5 eggs

Cook the mushrooms in a frying pan in a little butter, stirring frequently, until dry to the touch. Set aside.

Boil the red wine, thyme, garlic and shallots until reduced by two thirds. Meanwhile, melt the butter and keep warm.

Place the chicken livers in a food processor and purée with the salt and pepper. Add the eggs and purée again. While the processor is running add the warm melted butter and the wine reduction and purée for a further 2 minutes. Pass this mixture through a sieve into a large bowl. Whisk in the mushroom purée.

Line a terrine with Clingfilm and pour in the liver mixture. Cover with a lid, making sure not to fold the Clingfilm over. Put in a deep roasting tin, pour boiling water into the tin and cook in a preheated oven at 180°C/350°F/gas 4 for 40-45 minutes until set. Remove the terrine from the water and leave to cool completely before slicing.

Serves 14

And...   Mrs B's Sweet Piccalilli

1 cucumber, peeled, deseeded and diced
8 shallots, chopped
1kg/2lb peeled button onions
1 head of cauliflower, cut into tiny florets

3 red peppers, diced
salt
550ml/1pt white wine vinegar
1 1/2 tsp chopped chilli
350g/12oz caster sugar
50g/2oz mustard powder

25g/1oz ground turmeric
1 tbsp cornflour mixed with a little water
white pepper

Weigh all the prepared vegetables, except the red peppers, and add 25g/1oz salt per 450g/1lb vegetables. Put in to a colander over a bowl and leave for 3 hours.

Rinse the vegetables. Put the vinegar, chilli, sugar, mustard and turmeric into a large pan (not aluminium) and bring to the boil. Add the vegetables and cook until just tender.

Finally, stir in the red peppers and cornflour paste. Boil, stirring, until thick. Ladle into sterilised jars, and seal. Leave to cool. Store in a cool, dark, dry place for up to 6 months.

Makes 2l/3 1/3pt

THE STAGG INN
Titley, Herefordshire

In 2001, The Stagg Inn received the ultimate culinary accolade of a Michelin Star. It was a news story that alerted those few people still in the dark to the revolution that had been taking place in pub food over the past few years. Steve Reynolds runs the kitchen and Nicola Holland the front of house and together they have created one of the most exciting pub experiences in Britain. Rural and remote in deepest Herefordshire on the Welsh Borders, their philosophy is to source the excellent local produce that their beautiful location offers them.

Starter Crab Cakes

$1^1/2$ spring onions, chopped
1 tbsp olive oil
450g/1lb fresh crabmeat
40g/$1^1/2$oz white breadcrumbs
$1/2$ tbsp chopped parsley
$1^1/2$ tbsp chopped chives
$1/2$ tbsp chopped coriander
$1^1/2$ tbsp mayonnaise

$1/4$ tsp Dijon mustard
$1/4$ tsp English mustard powder
$1/4$ tsp Tabasco
salt
1 large egg yolk
salad and lemon, or a lemon
  beurre blanc, to serve

For the Coating
2 eggs beaten with a splash of
  milk
175g/6oz plain flour
115g/4oz fresh breadcrumbs

Fry the spring onions in half the olive oil to soften them slightly. Combine with the remaining ingredients until thoroughly mixed.

Divide into 8 portions and roll into balls. (If the mixture is difficult to handle add some more breadcrumbs.) Flatten into cakes and coat in beaten egg then the flour and breadcrumbs. Fry in olive oil until golden on both sides then put in a preheated oven at 190°C/375°F/gas 5 for 7 minutes.

Serve with salad and lemon, or a lemon beurre blanc.

Serves 4 as a starter or supper dish

Main	**Black Pudding Stuffed Tenderloin of Pork with Aubergine Sauce**

For the Sauce
4 shallots
1$^{1}/_{2}$ garlic cloves
4 tbsp olive oil
$^{1}/_{2}$ large aubergine, rubbed in
  salt, rinsed and dried
550ml/1pt red wine
550ml/1pt chicken stock

150ml/5fl oz double cream

2 tenderloins of free-range pork
  (preferably Tamworth)
75g/3oz of good quality black
  pudding, finely diced
1$^{1}/_{2}$ egg whites
salt and pepper

olive oil, for frying
1 tbsp butter

For the Rösti
2 potatoes (Wilja work well)
4 tbsp mild olive oil

To make the sauce, fry the shallots and garlic in the olive oil in a large stainless steel pan until soft. Turn up the heat then add the aubergine and cook until lightly coloured. Pour in the wine and reduce by two thirds. Add the chicken stock, reduce by half then add the cream and simmer gently for 5 minutes. Season to taste. Blend the entire mixture until smooth then set aside and keep warm.

Meanwhile, cut off the thin tail end from the tenderloins and set aside. Push a steel rod firmly through the centre of each tenderloin to give a hole about 2cm/$^{3}/_{4}$" in diameter. Chop up the trimmed-off tail ends and place in a food processor with salt and pepper. Pulse until smooth. Add the egg whites and pulse again until the mixture forms a ball. Put in a bowl, add the black pudding and combine thoroughly. Stuff this mixture into the tenderloins ensuring they are tightly packed.

Heat a frying pan, coat the base in olive oil then add the butter. Sprinkle the outside of the tenderloins with salt then colour on all sides in the pan. Place in a preheated oven at 190°C/375°F/gas 5 for 15 minutes.

To make the rösti, put the potatoes in a clean tea towel and squeeze out the water. Season and separate the potato strands. Divide into 4 portions. Heat a frying pan until smoking then add 1 tabllespoon olive oil. Add the potato portions and flatten each one with a spatula. (Cook in batches if necessary.) Put a knob of butter on top of each and cook until golden. Turn over and cook the other side. Keep warm while frying the remaining potato and until the pork is ready.

To serve, slice each tenderloin into 6 discs. Place a rösti in the centre of each plate and fan out 3 slices on each rösti. Spoon sauce around the rösti.

Serves 4

Dessert   Passion-fruit Jelly with Panacotta

25 passion-fruits, halved
150ml/5fl oz water
115g/4oz caster sugar
2 leaves of gelatine, soaked
  according to the packet
  instructions

4 passion-fruits, for decoration

For the Panacotta
300ml/^{1}/$_2$pt double cream
75ml/3fl oz full cream milk
75g/3oz caster sugar

seeds from 1 vanilla pod
1^1/$_2$ leaves of gelatine, soaked
  according to the packet
  instructions

Pass the passion-fruit through a sieve to remove the seeds.

Bring 150ml/5fl oz water and the sugar to the boil. Leave to cool for 5 minutes then whisk in the softened gelatine. Pour into 4 dariole moulds (or other small, round dishes) so that they are half-filled. Leave to set in the fridge for about 1 hour.

To make the panacotta, bring the cream, milk, sugar and vanilla seeds to the boil. Leave to cool for 5 minutes then whisk in the softened gelatine. Pour through a sieve into a jug and use to top up the moulds. Return to the fridge to set.

To serve, dip the moulds briefly in warm water then invert onto the plates. Scoop the seeds from half a passion-fruit over the top of the jelly and put the other half by the side. Decorate with extra fruit.

Serves 4

And...   Pigeon Breasts with Herb Risotto and Sage Sauce

For the Sauce
^{1}/$_2$ shallot, finely chopped
^{1}/$_2$ garlic clove, finely chopped
knob of butter
300ml/^{1}/$_2$pt chicken stock
2 sage leaves

For the Risotto
1 ^{1}/$_2$ small onion, finely
  chopped
^{1}/$_2$ garlic clove, finely chopped
50g/2oz butter, plus a knob to
  finish
100g/3^1/$_2$oz arborio rice

425ml/15fl oz chicken stock
15g/^{1}/$_2$oz grated Parmesan
1 tbsp chopped chives
salt and pepper
4 pigeon breasts, off the bone
  with skin on
olive oil, for frying

To make the sauce, fry the shallot and garlic in the butter until soft. Add the stock and boil until reduced by two thirds. Pass through a fine sieve. Return to the heat, add the sage and boil again until syrupy. Discard the sage before serving.

Meanwhile, make the risotto: sauté the onion and garlic in the butter until soft. Stir in the rice, then add 150ml/5fl oz of the stock. Simmer until almost all the stock has been absorbed, stirring occasionally. Repeat with another 150ml/5fl oz of stock. Add the final 150ml/5fl oz and repeat. Stir in the Parmesan, the chives, a knob of butter and season if necessary.

Warm a frying pan that can go in the oven. Sprinkle the pigeon breasts with salt and pepper if liked. Lay the breasts, skin side down, in the pan and colour lightly in olive oil. Turn the breasts over and place straight away in a preheated oven at 200°C/400°F/gas 6. Cook for 4 minutes so the breasts are pink in the centre. Leave to rest in a warm place for 2 minutes before thinly slicing the pigeon breasts then fan them out on top of a serving of risotto. Drizzle the sauce around.

Serves 4 as a starter or 2 as a main course

And...	**Pear Perry Sorbet**

Good to serve as a between-course palate cleanser or as an accompaniment to poached pears or chocolate puddings.

2 large pears, peeled, cored and
  roughly chopped
250g/9oz caster sugar

100ml/3$^{1}/_{2}$fl oz glucose syrup
500ml/18fl oz water

1$^{1}/_{2}$l/2$^{1}/_{2}$pt perry (we like
  Dunkerton's Organic)

Put the pears in a pan with the sugar and glucose syrup and 500ml/18fl oz water and bring to the boil. Simmer briskly for about 10 minutes until the pears are soft. Purée in a blender then add the perry.

Churn in a sorbetiere according to the manufacturer's instructions. Or place in the freezer and whisk every hour for 6 hours until the sorbet is smooth and set.

Makes 1l/1$^{3}/_{4}$pt

THE STAR INN
Lidgate, Suffolk

Since Maria Teresa Axon took over this attractive little village pub in 1993, its reputation has gone from strength to strength. Born in Barcelona, Maria Teresa comes from a family with a long tradition of first-class Catalan cuisine, not just in Barcelona but also in the Pyrenees and on the Catalan coast. This experience shows through in the menu at the pub which, whilst broadly Mediterranean, includes game dishes with obvious mountain heritage as well as a wide range of seafood dishes.

Main	Pimentos de Piquillos Rellenos con Brandada de Bacalao

12 piquillo peppers or 6 red
  peppers, roasted and peeled
650-750g/about 1¹/₂lb salt cod

(brandade), soaked
olive oil
400ml/14fl oz double cream

salt and pepper

Fill 8 piquillo peppers or 4 red peppers with the brandade and place in a lightly-oiled medium-sized baking dish. Bake in a preheated oven at 190°C/375°F/gas 5 for about 20 minutes. Before removing from the oven, check that the brandade stuffing is properly heated.

Meanwhile, purée the remaining peppers. Heat the cream almost to boiling, then stir in the purée, adding salt and pepper to taste.

Serve the stuffed peppers on the creamy purée.

Serves 4

Main	Baked Whole Sea Bass

300g/10oz potatoes, sliced
1 x 750g-1kg/1³/₄-2lb sea bass
2 tomatoes, halved
2 onions, sliced into rings

2 garlic cloves, crushed
leaves from 2 sprigs of
  rosemary, chopped
leaves from 2 sprigs of thyme,

chopped
salt and pepper
white wine

Blanch the potato slices in boiling water for 5 minutes. Drain and rinse in cold running water. Drain again.

Place the sea bass in a lightly oiled shallow baking dish, and put the potatoes around it. Arrange the tomatoes beside the fish with the onions on top of the potatoes. Sprinkle over the herbs and seasoning and add a fe glugs of wine. Bake in a preheated oven at 200°C/400°F/gas 6 for 30 minutes.

Serves 1-2

Dessert	**Cream Catalana**

500ml/18fl oz single cream
peel of 1 lemon peel, in a long

strip
1 cinnamon stick

3 egg yolks
175g/6oz sugar

Pour the cream into a saucepan and add the lemon peel and cinnamon stick. Bring to the boil, then take off heat and remove the lemon peel and cinnamon. Leave to cool.

Beat the egg yolks with one third of the sugar then stir in the cream. Pour back into the pan and cook over a low heat, stirring, until the custard thickens; do not allow to boil. Pour the custard into 4 ramekins almost to the brim. Leave to cool and set.

Sprinkle the remaining sugar over the tops of the custards. Lay a very hot skewer on the sugar to caramelise it. In Cataluna special branding irons are sold for this purpose. The sugar can also be caramelised to a rich brown colour under a hot grill.

Serves 4

And...	**Pollo a la Sanfaina**

$2^1/_2$kg/$5^1/_2$lb chicken, cut into
   8 pieces
olive oil, for basting

salt and pepper
mixed fresh herbs, chopped
water, about 2 wine glasses

1.5l/$2^3/_4$pt ratatouille, made to
   your favourite recipe
sautéed potatoes, to serve

Baste the chicken with olive oil and season with salt and pepper and the herbs. Roast in a preheated oven at 200°C/400°F/gas 6 for $1^1/_4$-$1^1/_2$ hours.

Remove the chicken from the roasting tin. Pour off the fat in the dish and stir a couple of wine glasses of water into the tin. Add the ratatouille then put the chicken on top. Simmer for a short while to ensure that both the chicken and ratatouille are hot. Serve with sautéed potatoes.

Serves 4

TROUBLE HOUSE INN
Tetbury, Gloucestershire

Prior to moving to The Trouble House Inn at Tetbury in Gloucestershire, Michael Bedford worked in the kitchens of one of the world's greatest chefs, Pierre Koffman, at his superlative restaurant, La Tante Claire, in London. Koffman's influence lives with him to this day and, as with Koffman, Michael is dedicated to producing food full of flavour and true to its ingredients. He and his wife, Sarah, only took over the pub in late 2000. They made their mark immediately and are now enjoying the fruits of their labours with enthusiastic devotees coming from far and wide.

Starter | Ravioli of Mushroom with an Onion Cappucino

For the Onion Cappucino
2 English onions, roughly chopped
100g/$3^1/_2$oz butter
salt and pepper
300ml/$^1/_2$pt double cream
300ml/$^1/_2$pt milk
300ml/$^1/_2$pt chicken stock

For the Mushroom Filling
50ml/2fl fl oz oil
18 mushrooms, coarsely chopped
5 shallots, chopped
50g/2oz unsalted butter
1 bunch of flat parsley, chopped
2 cloves garlic, crushed

salt and pepper

200g/7oz pasta dough
1 egg yolk
60g/2oz basil purée (see note)

Note: For the basil purée, boil a bunch of basil in salted water, refresh in iced water then liquidise with a pinch of Parmesan, and add a few teaspoons of olive oil.

Sweat the onion in butter for 30 minutes until soft and almost pulped. Add salt, pepper, cream, milk and chicken stock and simmer for 20 minutes. Liquidise and put in a saucepan.

To make the filling, heat the oil in a sauté pan until very hot and then add the mushrooms and sear for a few minutes. Add the shallots and butter. When the shallots have softened add the parsley, garlic, salt and pepper. Leave to cool.

Roll out the pasta on a machine until almost thin enough to see through. Divide into 8 pieces. Put 2 dessertspoons of mushroom mix on the centre of the pasta sheet. Brush egg yolk around the mix then fold over the remaining pasta and press the whole ravioli in between both hands, squeezing out the air bubbles and sealing the mushrooms inside. Cook in boiling water with salt and oil for 2 minutes then plunge into iced water and reserve.

To serve, blitz the sauce to a froth, pour it over the pasta and garnish with basil purée.

Serves 4

Main	**Coq-au-vin**

12 chicken legs
4 onions, finely diced
200g/7oz smoked bacon
  trimmings
1l/1^3/$_4$pt red wine
200g/7oz flour
120ml/4fl oz oil
5-6 cloves garlic, chopped

1 bouquet garni, wrapped in
  leek leaves
2l/3^1/$_2$pt veal stock
salt and pepper

For the Garnish
200g/7oz bacon lardons,
  blanched

200g/7oz button mushrooms
200g/7oz button onions, peeled
  and blanched
80ml/2fl^1/$_2$oz oil
parsley, chopped

Marinate the chicken legs, onions and bacon overnight in red wine. Drain the legs and reserve the wine. Coat the legs in flour, shake off any excess and fry in 80ml/2^1/$_2$fl oz of oil until golden brown. Caramelise the bacon and onion in a thick-bottomed pot with the rest of the oil. Add the chicken, garlic, bouquet garni, wine and veal stock to the onion and bacon. Bring to the boil, skim and simmer for two hours. Remove the chicken legs and pass the stock through a chinoise, then reduce to a glossy sauce. Adjust seasoning, pour over the legs and reserve.

Fry the lardons, mushrooms and onions in oil and add to the chicken legs. Garnish with parsley.

Serves 6

Dessert	**English Raspberries in Red Wine and Thyme**

2 bottles red wine (Australian
  Shiraz is a good choice)

sugar to taste
6 punnets of raspberries

1 bunch of thyme

Boil the wine and sugar together, take off the heat, add the raspberries and thyme. Chill for 24 hours.

Serves 8

And...   Reblochon with Roast Tomatoes

olive oil
1/2 baguette, sliced very thinly on the diagonal, into 8 slices
500g/1lb 2oz Reblochon cheese, divided into 24 wedges

15 vine-ripened baby tomatoes
50g/2oz rocket
50g/2oz curly endive
50g/2oz small spinach leaves
50g/2oz radicchio
1 Little Gem lettuce, divided into leaves

50g/2oz basil leaves
leaves from 1/2 bunch flat leaf parsley

Drizzle a little olive oil over the bread and bake in a preheated oven at 220°C/425°F/gas 7 for 3 minutes. Lower the oven temperature to 200°C/400°F/gas 6. Put 3 wedges of cheese on each slice of bread and put on a baking sheet. Add the tomatoes onto the baking sheet and bake for 4 minutes, until the cheese starts to run.

Mix the salad and basil leaves. Season with a little olive oil and toss with the leaves. Put the salad in the centre of a bowl. Place the cheese toasts on top with the tomatoes on the side. Drizzle with olive oil and serve.

Serves 4

And...   Coffee Jam Doughnuts

5g/1/4oz fresh yeast
25g/1oz caster sugar
about 125ml/4 1/2fl oz mixed milk and water
50ml/2fl oz espresso coffee

200g/7oz strong white flour
pinch of salt
1 egg, beaten
50g/2oz margarine, melted
jam

oil, for deep frying
caster sugar mixed with a little ground cinnamon, for coating

Dissolve the yeast and sugar in a little of the liquid. Sift the flour and salt into a bowl and make a well in the centre. Pour in the yeast liquid, sprinkle with a little salt and cover with a clean cloth. Leave in a warm place until the yeast ferments.

Stir in the egg, the margarine, the remaining liquid and the coffee and knead well to form a smooth dough that is free from stickiness. Cover and put in a warm place until doubled in volume.

Divide the dough into 8 pieces and mould each one into a ball. Press a floured thumb into each ball and put in a little jam. Mould carefully to seal in the jam. Put on a well floured tray, cover again and leave until puffy.

Heat a deep pan, half filled with oil, to about 175°C/340°F. Add the doughnuts in batches and fry for 12-15 minutes until golden. Drain well before rolling in the cinnamon-flavoured caster sugar.

Makes 8

THE VILLAGE PUB
Barnsley, Gloucestershire

The Cotswolds has many picture perfect villages and Barnsley is no exception. Rosemary Verey's garden is here and so, of course, is The Village Pub. Dominic Blake's award-winning cooking attracted attention the moment that landlords Rupert Pendered and Tim Haigh put the final touches to the revamped, refurbished old pub. It is now a place of sophistication and relaxation, serving food of the very highest standards yet still managing to retain the feel of a traditional country pub.

Starter | Wild Garlic Soup

2 garlic cloves, crushed
1 large onion, finely chopped
2 tbsp olive oil
1l/1$\frac{3}{4}$pt chicken or

vegetable stock
1 large potato, cut into
1.2cm/$\frac{1}{2}$" cubes
1 tsp paprika

1 bunch of wild garlic, shredded
salt and pepper
croutons, to serve

Cook the garlic and onion in the olive oil in a saucepan over a low heat until soft. Add the stock, potato and paprika. Bring to the boil then simmer until the potatoes are tender. Add the wild garlic and cook for 1 minute (no longer otherwise the colour will dull).

Cool the soup slightly then purée in a blender. Pour through a medium sieve and reheat gently. Adjust the seasoning and serve with croutons.

Serves 6

Main | Roast Hake, Clam and Bacon Chowder

50 Palourde clams, washed and
  scrubbed
1 large onion, finely chopped
2 leeks, white part only, cut into
  1.2cm/$\frac{1}{2}$" dice
vegetable oil, for cooking

8 slices streaky bacon, cut into
  thin strips
2 garlic cloves, finely chopped
350ml/12fl oz white wine
2 bay leaves
300g/10oz potatoes, diced

400ml/14fl oz double cream
salt and pepper
4 x 150-200g/5-7oz hake
  steaks, skin and bone still on
1 bunch of chives, finely
  chopped

Place the clams in a large pan with a splash of water, cover tightly and cook over a high heat. When the clams have just opened, tip into a muslin-lined colander over a bowl. Save the liquid in the bowl.

Cook the onion and leeks in the oil over a low heat until soft. Add the bacon and garlic and cook for 1 minute. Pour in the white wine and reduce to a syrup. Add the bay leaves, potatoes and clam liquid and simmer until the potatoes are just tender. Stir in the cream and cook for 2 minutes.

Meanwhile, heat a non-stick frying pan, add 1 tablespoon of vegetable oil and quickly brown the hake steaks on both sides. Put the fish in a greased, shallow baking dish and bake in a preheated oven at 180°C/350°F/gas 4 for about 12 minutes until the flesh just flakes when tested with the point of a sharp knife.

Add the clams to the chowder and heat through gently. Adjust the seasoning, if necessary.

Put a piece of hake in each warmed serving bowl and spoon on the chowder. Sprinkle with the chopped chives and serve.

Serves 4

Dessert | Raspberry and Elderflower Jelly

3 sheets of gelatine	450ml/16fl oz hot water	250g/9oz ripe raspberries
35g/1½oz caster sugar	150ml/5fl oz elderflower cordial	double cream, to serve

Soak the gelatine according to the packet instructions.

Stir the sugar into hot water until dissolved. Add the gelatine and elderflower cordial and stir together well. Divide half the jelly among 6 wine glasses, half filling them. Leave in the fridge for 1 hour to set. Keep the remaining jelly at room temperature so that it remains liquid.

Divide the raspberries among the glasses, then top up with the remaining jelly. Return to the fridge until set. Serve with double cream.

Serves 6

And... | Pickled Cherries

30 cherries	1 clove	finely chopped
50ml/2fl oz rice wine vinegar	1 tsp black peppercorns	225ml/8fl oz water
100g/3½oz caster sugar	1 small chilli, deseeded and	

Put all ingredients into a saucepan, and bring to the boil. Cool slightly then transfer to a clean, airtight storage jar. Store in the fridge for up to 4-5 days.

Serve with terrines or cold sliced ham.

And...   Roast Mushroom, Bacon and Mozzarella Sandwich

12 flat mushrooms, peeled and
  stalks removed
knob of butter
salt and pepper

8 slices unsmoked streaky
  bacon
4 slices of sourdough bread
1 bunch of rocket

1 x 150g/5oz mozzarella, cut
  into 4 slices
olive oil, for drizzling

Lay the mushrooms, curved side down, in a shallow baking dish and smear butter over them. Season and bake in a preheated oven at 180°C/350°F/gas 4 for about 15 minutes, basting occasionally, until tender.

Meanwhile, grill the bacon until crisp.

Toast the bread on both sides and divide the rocket among the 4 slices. Top with mushroom, 3 per person, then bacon and sliced mozzarella. Drizzle with olive oil and season lightly. Warm under grill until cheese is melted. Serve straight away.

Serves 4

PUB ADDRESSES

THE ANGEL INN
Hetton, North Yorkshire BD23 6LT
Phone 01756 730263
Fax 01756 730363
E-mail info@angelhetton.co.uk

Head Chef Bruce Elsworth
Chef Director John Topham

THE ATLAS
16 Seagrave Road, London SW6
Phone 020 7385 9129
Fax 020 7386 9113

Chefs George Manners,
Fatiha Gorieze, Clare O'Hallaran

BURTS HOTEL
Market Square, Melrose
Scotland TD6 9PL
Phone 01896 822285
Fax 01896 822870
E-mail burtshotel@aol.com

Head Chef Gary Moore

THE CHOLMONDELEY ARMS
Cholmondeley, Bickley Moss
Cheshire SY14 8HN
Phone 01829 720300
Fax 01829 720123
E-mail
cholmondeleyarms@cwcom.net

Head Chef Carolyn Ross-Lowe

THE COW SALOON BAR AND DINING ROOM
89 Westbourne Park Road
London W2 5QH
Phone 020 7221 5400
Fax 020 7727 8687
E-mail
thecow@thecow.freeserve.co.uk

Head Chef James Rix

THE CRICKETERS
Clavering, Essex CB11 4QT
Phone 01799 550442
Fax 01799 550882
E-mail cricketers@lineone.net

Head Chef Raymond Sexton
Pastry Chef Justin Greig

THE CROWN
223 Grove Road
London E3 5SN
Phone Bar 020 8981 9998
Phone Office 020 8983 5832
E-mail sb@singhboulton.co.uk

Recipes by Caroline Hamlin

THE DUKE OF CAMBRIDGE
30 St Peter's Street
London N1 8JT
Phone Bar 020 7359 3066
Phone Office 020 7359 9450
E-mail sb@singhboulton.co.uk

Head Chef Caroline Hamlin

THE EAGLE
159 Farringdon Road
London EC1R 3AL
Phone 020 7837 1353
Fax 020 7689 5882

Head Chef
Tom Norrington Davies

THE EAGLE AND CHILD
Maltkiln Lane
Bispham Green
Lancashire L40 3SG
Phone 01257 462297
Fax 01257 464718

Head Chef John Mansfield

THE EAGLE AND CHILD
The Royalist Hotel, Digbeth Street
Stow-on-the-Wold
Gloucestershire GL54 1BN
Phone 01451 830670
Fax 01451 870048
E-mail
info @theroyalisthotel.co.uk

Head Chef Alan Thompson

THE FOX
28 Paul Street, London EC2
Phone 020 7729 5708
E-mail fox.ph@virgin.net

Chefs Trish Hilferty, Harry Lester

THE FOX AND HOUNDS
66 Latchmere Road
Battersea, London SW11 2JU
Phone 020 7924 5483
Fax 020 7738 2678

Head Chef George Manners
Chef Edward Mottershaw

THE FOX INN
Lower Oddington
Nr. Moreton-in-Marsh
Gloucestershire GL56 0UR
Phone 01451 870555
Fax 01451 870669
E-mail info@foxinn.net

Head Chef Ray Pearce

THE GRIFFIN INN
Fletching,
East Sussex TN22 3SS
Phone 01825 722890
Fax 01825 722810

Head Chef Jason Williams

THE HAVELOCK TAVERN
57 Masbro Road
London W14 0LS
Phone 020 7603 5374
Fax 020 7602 1163

Head Chef Jonny Haughton

THE HOSTE ARMS
The Green, Burnham Market
Norfolk PE31 8HD
Phone 01328 738777
Fax 01328 730103
E-mail
  reception@hostearms.co.uk

Head Chef Andrew McPherson

THE HUNDRED
  HOUSE HOTEL
Bridgnorth Road
Norton, Shropshire TF11 9EE
Phone 01952 730353
Fax 01952 730355
E-mail
  hundredhouse@lineone.net

Head Chef Stuart Phillips

THE IVY HOUSE
London Road, Chalfont St Giles
Buckinghamshire HP8 4RS
Phone 01494 872184
Fax 01494 872870

Head Chef Jane Mears

THE JOLLY SPORTSMAN
Chapel Lane, East Chiltington
Sussex BN7 3BA
Phone 01273 890400
Fax 01273 890400
E-mail
  jollysportsman@onetel.net.uk

Head Chef Richard Willis

NANTYFFIN CIDER MILL
Brecon Road
Crickhowell
Powys, Wales NP8 1SG
Phone 01873 810775

Head Chef Sean Gerrard

THE NEW INN AT COLN
Coln St-Aldwyns
Cirencester
Gloucestershire GL7 5AN
Phone 01285 750651
Fax 01285 750657
E-mail stay@new-inn.co.uk

Head Chef Alistair Ward

THE NOBODY INN
Doddiscombsleigh
Devon EX6 7PS
Phone 01647 252394
Fax 01647 252 978
E-mail info@nobodyinn.co.uk

Chef Paul Tait

THE PEAR TREE
Top Lane
Whitley
Wiltshire SN12 8QX
Phone 01225 709131
Fax 01225 702276

Head Chef Mark Nacchi

THE PELICAN
45 All Saints Road
London W11 1HE
Phone Bar 020 7792 3073
Phone Office 020 7792 0936
E-mail sb@singhboulton.co.uk

Head Chef Karen Kennedy

PENHELIG ARMS
Terrace Road
Aberdyfi
Gwynedd
Wales LL35 0LT
Phone 01654 767215
Fax 01654 767690
E-mail
  penheligarms@saqnet.co.uk

Head Chef Jane Howkins

QUEEN'S HEAD HOTEL
Troutbeck
Windermere
Cumbria LA23 1PW
Phone 015394 32174
Fax 015394 31938

Head Chef Wallace Drummond

THE RED LION
By the Bridge
Burnsall
North Yorkshire
Phone 01756 720204
Fax 01756 720292
E-mail redlion@daelnet.co.uk

Head Chef Jim Rowley

THE RIVERSIDE INN
  AND RESTAURANT
Aymestrey
Herefordshire HR0 9ST
Phone 01568 708440
Fax 01568 709058
E-mail
  riverside@aymestrey.fsnet.co.uk

Head Chef André Cluzeau

(continued overleaf)

THE ROEBUCK INN
Brimfield
Ludlow
Shropshire SY8 4NE
Phone 01584 711230
Fax 01584 711654
E-mail
  dave@roebuckinn.demon.co.uk

Chefs David Willson-Lloyd,
  Jonathan Waters

THE ROYAL OAK
The Square
Yattendon
Berkshire RG18 0UG
Phone 01635 201325
Fax 01635 201926

Head Chef Jason Galdwin

SEAFOOD BAR
& RESTAURANT
16 West End
St Monans
Scotland KY10 2BX
Phone 01333 730327
Fax 01333 730327

Head Chef Craig Millar
Sous Chef Kevin McElhinnie

THE SPREAD EAGLE
Sawley
Forest of Bowland
Nr Clitheroe
Lancashire BB7 4NH
Phone 01200 441202
Fax 01200 441973

Head Chef Greg Barnes

THE STAR INN
Lidgate
Newmarket
Suffolk CB8 9PP
Phone 01638 500275

Head Chef Maria-Teresa Axon

THE STAGG INN
& RESTAURANT
Titley
Kington
Herefordshire HR5 3RL
Phone 01544 230221
Fax 01544 230221
E-mail
  reservations@thestagg.co.uk

Head Chef Steve Reynolds

TROUBLE HOUSE INN
Cirencester Road
Tetbury
Gloucestershire GL8 8SG
Phone 01666 502206
Fax 01666 504508

Head Chef Michael Bedford

THE VILLAGE PUB
Barnsley
Cirencester
Gloucestershire GL7 5EF
Phone 01285 740421
Fax 01285 740142
E-mail
  reservations@villagepub.co.uk

Head Chef Dominic Blake

INDEX